HOW TO WORK
WITH
CHURCH GROUPS

HOW TO WORK

WITH

CHURCH GROUPS

Mary Alice Douty

ABINGDON PRESS
NEW YORK — NASHVILLE

Library of Congress Catalog Card Number: 57-5076

SET UP, PRINTED, AND BOUND BY THE
PARTHENON PRESS. AT NASHVILLE,
TENNESSEE, UNITED STATES OF AMERICA

Blest be the tie that binds
  Our hearts in Christian love:
The fellowship of kindred minds
  Is like to that above.

—JOHN FAWCETT

STATEMENT OF PURPOSE

This book is meant for all leaders of groups in the local church. It is the outgrowth of many years of working with such groups, of teaching in leadership education classes, and of studying and experimenting in the field of group techniques. It is an attempt to put the principles of group work and of democratic group leadership into practical terms for the average church-school teacher or leader. Throughout the book illustrations are based on situations I have seen in action.

The first chapter, with its "Measuring Stick" for evaluation, gives a quick look at a variety of working group situations at all age levels. The second chapter states objectives in Christian education and some of the principles we know about how learning takes place. It emphasizes that much of our learning takes place in group situations. We need to understand teaching and learning, but beyond that we need an understanding of group interactions and group functioning. These two chapters are meant to set the stage.

The next four chapters deal with group patterns, group organization, understandings, procedures, and techniques for good group functioning. Attention is given to the role of the leader and his preparations, to helping the group understand its role, and to the techniques of getting and giving participation.

Chapters Seven, Eight, and Nine deal with three specific

elements in the total church-school program—recreation, drama, and choral speaking—looking at them as group activities, applying to them the principles of group work, and raising questions of purpose and accomplishment. The emphasis is on how we plan with groups and how we may help a group to function more effectively.

Chapter Ten looks at church-school superintendents, ministers, and directors of Christian education as leaders of groups of workers. It attempts to show how we can develop in that core of individuals a powerful fellowship of colaborers. Five guidelines for group leaders are given. The importance of group-work techniques is stressed in the light of the emphases on Christian family life, democracy, and world brotherhood.

This book may be used by one teacher in a program of self-improvement, or by a local church staff in a study group, or in a leadership education course on "Learning the Skills of Group Leadership."

MARY ALICE DOUTY

8

CONTENTS

CONTENTS

CHAPTER I

GROUPS AT WORK

THE SUNDAY MORNING AIR WAS CRISP AND CLEAR. THE SUN shone brightly from a brilliant blue sky, picking out the hints of autumn in the foliage of the trees. It was a brisk day, a glad day, a fitting day in which to sing the Creator's praise. The clangor of church bells found eager response as groups of worshipers moved toward the open doors.

Car after car drove up and parked, bringing parents, grandparents, and assorted sizes and ages of children. Clean, smiling faces and best Sunday dress belied the morning's struggle at home. Here were family groups who found it good to come together to learn and to worship.

A station wagon drove up, unloaded ten children, and left. These were from a residential section some distance away. The parents had organized a car pool so that they might send their children to the church. Yet it cannot be said that the children's families were left at home. The children carried their families with them in their attitudes, their habits, and their customs.

Across a vacant lot moved a gang of junior boys, joking and jostling as they came. Like puppy dogs they covered as much distance sideways as they did forward in moving toward the church. Most of their families came the few blocks in cars, but the boys walked, calling to one another along the way. They spied their teacher approaching the church and broke into a mad race to reach him first. Laughing and talking, they crowded into the doors together.

Down at the corner two high-school girls and a fellow stood talking. Other young people joined them. When a good crowd had gathered, they moved slowly into the church school.

How different is each person, and yet how important to each is his own particular group. We live and work and play for the most part in groups. We find pleasure in doing things with our friends. We give and take as we share our thoughts and our personalities. We do this or that because our friends like it or our families expect it. When a family or a group teams up on a project, things happen. It is important that church-school teachers learn the rules of working with groups.

This is a fairly new field of study. In the past quarter century research has revealed much about interpersonal relationships and group dynamics. Educators, businessmen, social workers, clubwomen, politicians, recreation leaders, are all making use of the best that is known about individuals in groups. Every church on a Sunday morning has within its walls as widely diverse a set of groups as will be found anywhere. In age the groups range from near infancy to octogenarians. Groups differ in size, purpose, and way of working. They have changing needs and growing abilities. A trip through an active church school will reveal to the perceptive observer a wide variety of group experiences and group maturities.

The following questions may form a helpful guide for profitable observation. We will use them in this chapter to guide our thinking as we look, through words, at a church school whose counterpart may be found in rural America,

---

A Measuring Stick
for Observing Groups at Work

1. What distinctive characteristics can we see in each age group?
2. What learnings are going on?
3. What is the relationship between teacher and class?
4. What evidence is there that the pupils are mentally active?
5. How much of the talking is done by the teacher?
6. Are the pupils following directions, or sharing actively in the planning and the work?
7. How much responsibility are the pupils taking?
8. What purposeful activities can we see?
9. Do pupils and teachers seem to enjoy what they are doing?

---

at the crossroads, and in the cities and towns throughout our land.

Before starting a similar journey in your own church, it would be well to recall some rules for visitors. As a visitor you look and listen, but you do not talk or touch. Make note of any comment, question, or idea that occurs to you and share it later. Be as inconspicuous as possible. Whether you approve or disapprove of what is going on, keep your facial expression pleasant. Enter and leave the room quietly. Here we go.

The Nursery Department

This is a pleasant room. Sunlight streams in through brightly draped windows. The floor is clean, linoleum with a checkered pattern. Chairs are small and tables are low. Three-year-olds, however, have little use for chairs. Most of the children are on the floor. One young towhead, engineering a train, almost runs us down. He looks up inquiringly from the strange feet to the strange faces, then rushes his train off across the room. In one corner a gracious three-year-old lady is serving tea in her best grown-up manner. The young lad at the table stirs his empty cup vigorously and drinks noisily. Children are busy at books, toys, blocks, dolls, and pegboards. Two of the three teachers move quietly around the room, joining in the conversation or play wherever opportunity arises. The third teacher, holding a picture, sits on a small chair. Three children bend over it, touching it, listening to the teacher, and talking. They remain with her several minutes. Two other children push their way in to see the picture, and the first three leave.

A sharp yell startles us. Turning, we see Chris with the train clutched under one arm. The other hand, half-raised, holds a block. In front of him, Jimmy weeps, holding his wounded head. Most of the children look but otherwise ignore the incident. Susie, who plays with Jimmy during the week, puts an arm around him and takes him to the book table. The weeping subsides. The teacher removes the block from Chris, saying quietly, "Blocks are for building, Chris." Chris hasn't moved nor have his eyes left Jimmy. Now he goes to the book table and stands looking curiously at Jimmy and Susie and the book.

Three notes on the piano tell the children that it is time to put the toys away. Ralph, who is almost four, rushes busily around, grabbing toys out of children's hands in his efforts to clean up. The teacher directs his energies toward some discarded toys on the floor. Most of the children help. Three of the youngest continue playing, oblivious to everything. As the teachers draw the children into a circle with a song, we take our leave.

Out in the hall we pause before going on to the kindergarten department. We reread the questions we were to keep in mind during our visit. What meanings can we take from what we have just seen?

Where are three-year-olds in group development? For most of them this is the first experience in life beyond the home and removed from mother's watchful eye. Is this beginning a happy experience? Is it laying a strong foundation for learning to love their neighbors?

The Kindergarten Department

The four- and five-year-olds, listening to a story, are gathered about a teacher. Three other teachers sit with the group. This room also has toys and books, small tables and chairs, a record player, and a bouquet of yellow chrysanthemums on a low table at the front. The teacher holds a large picture from which she is telling a story. Her speech moves rhythmically, her voice rising and falling. Her eyes move around the group as she speaks directly to one then another. Every child seems to be completely absorbed in the story. As it comes to an end, a sigh rises from the group. The teacher waits for the children's comments.

"That was a good story. I liked it."

"Me too. I liked the part where the camels got a drink."

"I saw some camels in the zoo this summer."

"I went to the zoo and I saw lions and tigers and everything."

15

The teacher breaks in hastily. "Who can tell us what a camel looks like?"

Several children describe camels, and the teacher, pointing to the picture, gets most of the group back from the zoo. "Why do you think Rebecca gave the camels a drink?"

"Because they were thirsty."

"Because they had a long trip."

"Because she was kind."

"Would you like to play the story?" Eager assent rises. Of course they would! This is a familiar activity often used to help the children feel the meaning of a story. Very quickly each teacher gathers a few children around her.

In the group near us a little girl named Becky takes charge. Playing a story is a common experience, and initiative has apparently been encouraged. "This will be the well," she says, placing two chairs back to back. "And you can be a camel, and you and you. Leslie, you be the man who brings the camels. And, Mary, you be my maid."

"I want to be Rebecca," protests Mary. Leslie meanwhile starts driving his camels around.

"No, I'm going to be Rebecca. You be that other lady in the picture."

"Maybe we'll have time for each of you to be Rebecca," says the teacher, restoring peace. The play proceeds, with the camels gratefully saying "thank you" each time they receive a drink.

Gradually the action subsides. We notice that each teacher is talking with her group about kindness as the children have experienced it themselves. Ideas about how we may be kind are shared. Someone volunteers to take the morning leaflet to a friend who is sick. Many children think of giving their

16

own pets a drink. Of course, Johnny wants a drink right now and so does Bill. They agree to wait until the session is over.

We step into the hall. Over the drinking fountain we compare notes and think about our guiding questions. What learnings were taking place? Was there evidence that these children are learning to take responsibility, that they are thinking and planning? Have the growing abilities of the children changed the character of group life to any extent?

The Primary Department

In the primary department we find the children in six small classes, two first, two second, and two third-grade groups. Several classes are meeting in the department room, but the superintendent directs us to one which is meeting in the kitchen. Like most churches this one is overcrowded and uses every inch of space.

"Well, I think we've got to write him a letter and tell him we want to come see him." The little girl is speaking emphatically as we enter. Several others nod agreement.

"We ought to tell him what we're studying about."

"And then tell him what questions we want to ask him."

"And when we want to see him."

It is obvious that the children are in accord and ready for action. The teacher takes out a large sheet of paper and a pen.

"All right," she says. "Go ahead." As the children dictate, she writes the letter in clear print. Every eye watches each movement of the pen. This is the letter:

Dear Mr. Jones:

We are the second-grade class and we are studying about the church. We want to know what a minister does besides preach

17

and pray. We would like to come to your office and ask you next Sunday morning at ten o'clock. Could we please?

> Your friends,
> Mrs. Russell's Class

"Would you all like to put your names at the bottom of the letter?" asks Mrs. Russell. They would indeed! Eager hands reach for the pen and paper. Mrs. Russell addresses the envelope and soon the letter, with ten names on it, is tucked inside. "Now whom shall we send to put the letter on Mr. Jones's desk where he will see it first thing in the morning?"

The little girl who had been so emphatic as we entered the room speaks again: "I think David should go because it was his idea in the first place to visit the minister."

The others nod in agreement. Robert volunteers, "I know where the office is. I could go along and show David where."

"Aw, I know where it is too." David speaks as if he thinks Robert's offer is an attempt to chisel in.

"You could take one person with you if you wanted to, David," says Mrs. Russell. An electric charge could not have set off a more instantaneous reaction. Every hand shoots toward David in the eagerness to be chosen. He surveys the field calmly enjoying his moment of power to the fullest.

At last he speaks. No judge ever pronounced sentence to a more attentive courtroom. "I think I'll take Sally."

Robert utters a noise of disgust, but the others accept the decision philosophically. Sally, who had suggested David, rises without a word and the two leave the room, faces intent.

We find this a convenient time to leave also. The guide questions tumble over each other in our minds as we think about these children. Learning? Enjoyment? Responsibility?

18

Purposeful activity? Planning? Relationships? The time was brief but we saw much. Pushing on toward the junior department, we wonder what distinctive characteristics we may see in the nine-to-eleven-year group.

The Junior Department

The junior classes are all crowded into one room. At the far end of it five boys and girls are arranging a worship center —a small table with a picture of Jesus, an open Bible, and a plain wooden cross. A quiet hubbub rises from the five little huddles of classes at work all around the room. The group at the far end turns out to be a worship committee. We sit down near enough to hear their final planning for the worship service which is to follow at the close of the morning session. The department superintendent is sitting with them. George, a tall sixth-grader, is chairman. He runs his hand through his hair and adjusts the unaccustomed tie on the white shirt self-consciously. Alan, a small fourth-grader with curly black hair and a finely chiseled face, is relating what he will say in the worship service.

"Well, I'm supposed to be Paul, and I'm going to tell them how I saw Jesus when I was going to Damascus. I think I ought to say that it was a wonderful experience and it changed my whole life."

"Couldn't you tell them you had been persecuting the Christians and now you weren't going to do it any more?" asks Jane.

"I don't know. I'm afraid I'd get stuck on that word persecution. Couldn't I just say that I joined the Christians and started some new churches?"

"Sure, that would be okay," says George. "Now let's see if we've got it all straight. I say the call to worship and an-

19

nounce the hymn. Then I read the Bible passage. Then you four tell what you remember about Jesus and Jane gives the prayer. Then . . ."

Jane interrupts. "Is this all right for the prayer, Mrs. Smith?" She gives her ideas in three or four sentences, suggesting that we all try to remember Jesus and follow him. Mrs. Smith says it sounds right to her. What about the others?

The committee agrees, but Susan has an addition. "You could say we're thankful for Jesus."

"Oh, sure, that's good," Jane agrees.

George continues: "After the prayer we have the offering and the response and then the closing hymn. That's all, isn't it?"

"What about the benediction?" asks Alan.

George rubs his chin and shifts in his chair. "Oh, yeah. I forgot that. How about you doing it?"

The younger boy is very solemn. This must be his first experience on a junior committee. "Well, I'll try. 'The Lord watch between me and thee'; is that it?"

"Yeah, that's okay. Well, I guess we're all set."

"It sounds very good to me. I'm proud of you. I'll be watch-ing the other boys and girls during the service to see if you really do make them think about Jesus. I believe you can if you think about them." Mrs. Smith's words seem to have the desired effect. The committee feels good about its work, but George and the others look around the room, thinking about the boys and girls whom they will lead in worship. "Dear God, help us to do a good job for you," is all the prayer the superintendent offers.

The committee members go to their classes. Here we have seen a group activity in which the children have shared the planning. One of their own number has acted as chairman of the committee. We wonder about the function of the teacher. She said very little. When a question was directed to her, she gave an opinion but then referred the matter to the boys and girls. She seemed to be just one of the group. Yet we know from our own experiences that responsibility such as we have seen in these children doesn't "just happen." This leader has apparently learned how to work with children in groups. We wish that we might see more, but there are other departments to visit. The morning is nearly half gone.

The Junior-High Department

These boys and girls—twenty or thirty of them—are all meeting together, singing a hymn. A teacher welcomes us and explains the situation. The group has a time for learning new hymns, choral speaking, and the like at the beginning of the morning. Sometimes they take up business for a few minutes. And they have worship before the class session, urging the boys and girls to go to the congregational worship after class. Just now there is a matter of business which one of the classes has asked permission to put before the whole group. Bob, a ninth-grader, is speaking.

"There are twenty-six of us here this morning, and there were twenty-five last Sunday morning. But only eight junior-highs came out to our Fellowship meeting last Sunday night. Now we think something is wrong and we've asked for time this morning to try to find out. We talked it over last Sunday night and we think there is a place for the Fellowship meeting. There are lots of things for us to do and not enough time in the morning session." He goes on to describe some of the things which the evening meeting could accomplish. "Now we want some discussion of this problem. And if the adults will pardon me, we want discussion from the junior-highs

21

only." His face gets red. "Now don't get me wrong. We're not putting the adults out. We just think the kids ought to speak first." He stops, shifts his position, coughs behind his hand, and waits.

One of the girls speaks. "Well, I wasn't there, Bob, because my family went for a drive out in the country and I went along."

"And I had too much homework," puts in a freckle-faced redhead. Several of his classmates laugh. Apparently they don't think too much of his study habits.

"I know everybody who didn't come had a good excuse," says Bob. "But we think if the Fellowship was going good, you'd make it your business to come. You wouldn't have excuses. The question is, what about the Fellowship?"

"Well, it's just not interesting. We never do anything."

"It's just like Sunday school all over—a worship service, somebody makes a talk, we sing a few songs, and that's it."

"And when we have a speaker, he's always too long winded."

The comments are sharp and to the point. Bob turns the conversation into more constructive channels. "You seem to have all the answers on what's wrong. How about some suggestions on things that would make the meetings good?"

The comments this time are equally sharp and to the point. The group wants to do things, make things, play games, have good discussion, put on a play. A seventh-grader wonders if his class can't work on their time line in the evening. "We never have time enough in the morning."

"We could work on our overseas relief project." Interest is keen. Bob gives everyone who wants a chance to speak. So far not an adult has spoken.

Now Bob gets a signal from the counselor. "Time is running away from us," Bob reminds the group. "What do you

22

say we continue this discussion this evening and set up the kind of Fellowship that everybody wants?"

Agreement is voiced throughout the room. "All right. Let's have no excuses. Everybody out and bring your ideas with you. And just to be sure we have a crowd, how about Mary getting a refreshment committee together and having something for us to eat?"

"I'll be here!" says the redhead, drawing another laugh.

"Tonight at seven then. And I hope all our teachers will come too. How about it? And thanks a lot for the time, Miss Jones."

The competence of this fourteen-year-old leaves us a bit breathless as we move on to the high-school department. We feel sure that all twenty-six will be at the meeting tonight and that a good Fellowship is on the way. We wonder about the adults' part in the proceedings. We have only a moment to think of the contrast between this and the function of adults in the other departments we have seen. And is Bob unusual? Do other junior-highs have the ability to lead discussions as he did? How can we develop or release such ability?

The Senior-High Department

The high-school youth meet in a rather small room. It is so crowded that we can scarcely get the door open. We can hear someone speaking, but it is impossible to get in. One of the girls steps out in the hall to see what we want.

"Oh," she exclaims in response to our statement that we are interested in finding out what they are doing. "I do wish you could get in to hear Professor Copeland. He's just wonderful. We've been studying a unit on our beliefs about the Bible and we've gotten into some awfully heated discussions.

23

He's a science professor at the college and a member of the church board. So we decided to ask him to tell us how he feels about the Bible. And golly, he's made it just about the most exciting book there ever was! And he's coming to our youth meeting tonight because he says he wants us to tell him how we feel about it. Boy, is that going to be a lively discussion!"

"Does everybody come to the evening meeting?" we ask.

"Oh yes, practically everybody. Plus some who don't come here in the morning."

"Do you have a good counselor?"

"Two of them—Mr. and Mrs. Donahue. They're with us both morning and evening. And we're with them half the week. I know we're a nuisance running in and out of their house, but they're so nice and they always seem so glad to see us. We're really lucky to have counselors like that."

We think so too. We apologize for interrupting. In her few brief sentences this student has given an enthusiastic picture of her group at work. Apparently adults have an important place in youth work. Two good counselors and an excellent resource person are highly appreciated. We have not seen enough to discover the ways in which the adults use their leadership. We have seen that the student who spoke with us has a strong sense of identification with her group and a feeling of its worth—at least in her thinking it is a good group. Again we wonder what makes it so. What are the laws or principles by which groups develop? So thinking, we move on.

Young-People's Department

"But my family needs food!" As we start to open the door, we hear a voice almost in tears. We wait outside, listening, hesitating to step in where such a pathetic plea is being made. The voice continues: "My husband is sick and he hasn't been able to work since we moved here. Now the children are hungry and the rent isn't paid."

"I can't help that," a harsh voice cuts the poor woman short. We look at each other in astonishment. Are we still in a Christian church? The man's voice goes on: "If we helped every transient that came along, we'd be swamped. The welfare department is here for our own citizens, and we haven't money enough for them. No, I can't help you at all."

"But what am I going to do?" the pitiful voice persists.

"Go on back where you came from. Or go to the Salvation Army. They don't ask any questions. Maybe they'll help you. I can't." A note of finality in the man's voice concludes the conversation and breaks the spell which had held us motionless outside the door. We push in, compelled to learn what is going on. We see no poverty-stricken women, no heartless welfare agent. We see a group of smiling young people, complimenting two of their number on a "performance well done." Role playing of course!

The discussion picks up where the dialogue stopped. The group is seated in a circle. There is joking that Marian should have gone on the stage instead of being a secretary. But attention quickly turns to the problem at hand.

Jack objects to the way Frank played the welfare agent. "Maybe you had to turn her down, but did you have to be so nasty about it?"

Frank laughs. "Well, maybe not, but I had to be definite. She could expect absolutely no help from the department."

"Why not?" Jack asks. Marian has the answer. She is particularly interested in this problem since she works as a secretary in the welfare office.

25

"Anyway, I don't see why we should pay taxes to support these foreigners who come here from other states and try to go on relief." Matt speaks vehemently, but a twinkle in his eyes suggests that he is simply trying to stir up a storm. He gets it.

"You can't just let people starve!"

"It wasn't Marian's fault that her husband got sick and couldn't work." This comment brings a laugh, but Marian picks it up.

"You know, I felt the way Matt spoke until I thought about this role I was to play. And it haunts me. What would I do if I were in that position? Where would I turn? We've got to find an answer!"

We hate to leave before they come to some conclusion, but we must go on if we are to see the young adults and the Bible class before the morning is over. We think again of our guide questions as we walk along. Yes, they apply to older people as well as to the children's departments. Here were enjoyment, purpose, responsibility, mental activity, planning, learning, good relationships. Every single question can be applied to help us evaluate this group. With such thoughts we enter the class for parents and other young adults.

The Young-Adult Class

This is the least attractive room we have been in all morning. A lovely vase of flowers attempts to brighten it, but cannot disguise the fact that this is a basement room with exposed pipes and a bare concrete floor. Yet a purposeful, even cheerful, atmosphere prevails. These young parents must have accepted this room in order that the children and youth might have more pleasant surroundings. A projector and screen

indicate that a film has been shown. The group is concluding a discussion of a family problem.

"I've certainly gotten something to think about this morning." A man in his early thirties speaks slowly, picking his
words carefully. "I always thought finances were the husband's problem. I'm still not sure that the kids ought to have
a share in making the family budget. But I'm going to have
to think about it."

"I know we haven't given enough thought to how we use
our money," says a young mother. "Right now I'm ashamed
of the way I gave the children their money for Sunday school
this morning. You can be sure we'll talk that over before next
Sunday."

Several others add their comments. We realize that this is
a group of adults who trust each other. They speak freely,
thoughtfully. Apparently they get help on their problems in
these weekly sessions.

Their relationships with each other are friendly, happy. In
the circle it is difficult to determine who is the leader. We
have seen several of the young adults taking responsibility,
guiding the discussion, and drawing others in. Certainly they
are all alert and interested. This is no group that sits back
and "lets George do it."

A young man announces the topic, still in the unit on Christian use of money, for next Sunday. He calls attention to the
help to be gained from the congregational worship at eleven
o'clock. We leave hastily, hoping to have at least a minute
or two in the Bible class.

The Bible Class

The rich carpeting, the fine draperies, and the comfortable
furniture tell us at once that this is the church parlor, a room

27

of some restraint. The atmosphere in the group is different too. These older folk sit comfortably in their chairs. The teacher expounds the lesson in a gracious and learned manner. He knows his Bible, and the students, listening and nodding, take pride in his knowledge. The bell rings, but they are in no hurry to leave. They sit patiently while he concludes the lesson. They join in the benediction, and class is over. Still the students seem in no hurry. They greet one another warmly as many small conversations spring up around the room. Several go to the teacher and take up some point in the lesson with him. He nods thoughtfully and listens to their comments.

We wonder about this group as we apply each of our guide questions to it. We do see some distinctive characteristics of this age. We note the lack of adults of middle years. The forties and fifties also have their distinctive characteristics. It is easy to see that they would not feel at home either in this group or in the young-adult group. Apparently there are good reasons for following the graded principle through the adult division.

We see many values in this group. The students seem to be interested in one another. There is a friendly atmosphere evident in their smiles, their conversation, and their easy approach to the teacher when the lecture is over. They show appreciation of his knowledge and they clearly enjoy being a part of this fellowship.

There is some evidence that the students are mentally active, since several of them discuss the lesson with the teacher after class. How much might the group have been enriched had this discussion been carried on with the whole group? Surely there are many capable persons here whose thinking would stimulate and challenge others. We do not sense that

28

this is a group hard at work on a problem. Is something vital lacking when thinking is not shared?

The Total Church

Looking around at the congregation in the morning service, we think of the total church. Here are the leaders of the woman's society, the members of the board, officials and trustees, the choir, recreation leaders, committee members—all the church family gathered in one act of corporate worship. The church is more than Sunday-morning study and worship. We have seen these people trying to relate their religion to everyday life. We read notices in the bulletin of the weekday and monthly activities. We see the names of those who carry responsibility for the organization and functioning of this church body.

We live in groups. In the church we work with groups. The importance of the group to the individual has been seen only in recent years. The group is now recognized as a most significant factor in the educational process. While each person is unique and has his own needs and abilities, one of his greatest needs is to find his place and build a satisfying relationship with others. The give and take of group life, the acceptance or rejection of the individual in it, the fellowship and response of related individuals are powerful influences which cannot be ignored. The church is primarily a group experience, and those who take an active part in the church are, in one way or another, leaders and members of groups. A study of group life and functioning is essential to anyone who would make his participation in the church effective.

CHAPTER II

SETTING THE FRAMEWORK

TALL, SLENDER SPIRE, REACHING INTO THE SKY—WHAT DOES it mean? Clangor of bells, pealing from the steeple—what do they say? People hurrying to the church—why do they come? Teacher, greeting his class with warmth—why does he teach?

Knowing our objectives, our purposes, comes first.

A group of leaders was asked to answer in a sentence or two the question, "Why do you teach?" Several of their answers may stimulate our own thinking about our purposes as leaders in the church.

"I teach a class of boys and girls because the teachers I had as a child meant so much to me," wrote one.

Another said, "My own children go to Sunday school, so I figure I have a duty to help with the teaching."

"The church has always been important in my life," wrote a youth counselor, "and I wouldn't feel right without a job."

"I get so much out of it myself," was another answer. "I'm sure church wouldn't mean so much to me without the preparation and responsibility that go with leadership in the church school."

All of these responses are good, but we need to search deeper. Whether our work be teaching, counseling, leading recreation, holding office, or any other of the many jobs of leadership in the church, we must face these questions: What are we trying to accomplish? Why do we teach?

Let us say it boldly. We are giving ourselves to God for the fulfillment of Jesus' prayer and ours, "Thy kingdom come." We choose to serve this King who draws us to himself through love. We find our highest joy, our deepest satisfaction, in his law and his will. Parents, teachers, the Church, the Bible, all help to lead us into that relationship with God where he is sovereign in our lives.

The other aspect of the kingdom of God in Jesus' teaching is not so immediate. It is the slow working of yeast in the dough. It is the tiny mustard seed growing into a large tree. It is the disciples of the Master going into the whole world to preach, to teach, and to heal.

We can state our objectives broadly in this way: We are trying to help men and women, boys and girls, to learn and to follow the teachings of Jesus. He gave two commandments! Love God. Love your neighbor. So simply put; yet it takes a lifetime of devotion and practice to learn and to live them!

It is our concern as teachers of the Christian religion to help our students to grow in their understanding of God and of the teachings of Jesus. We search the Bible and study the lives of men of good will. We think and meditate upon what we read and see. We stretch our minds by sharing our thoughts with one another. Alone and together we struggle to develop our beliefs and our philosophy.

By their fruits are they known, said Jesus. And we try to help our students express these beliefs in daily actions and habits. Religious living is not knowledge of facts or memorization of scripture, helpful though these may be. It is the little daily acts of kindness and thoughtfulness that indicate the religion we have learned. It is the attitude we show toward

31

other people. It is our concern for the downtrodden, the sick, the discouraged people about us. And it is the calm, the radiance, the joy that shines on the face of one who walks in fellowship with an all-wise, all-powerful, all-loving God.

We teach toward commitment to God and to the work of God through the Church. We try to develop citizens who look at politics, economics, society, with the teachings of Jesus in mind. Honesty in government, welfare of migrants, rights of minorities, relief to the stricken—these are proper concerns of Christians, both locally and world wide. Our missionaries today study medicine, dentistry, agriculture, economics, education, politics, sociology, and science. It is our creed that God is the Father of all, that all men are brothers. Our brother's need, his disease, his hunger, his subjection are our concern. We minister to his soul and to his body.

And in our teaching in the Church we think of family life. Here it is perhaps hardest, and should be easiest, to live as Christians. The mother-father relationship toward the children, the parent relationship of boys and girls, should these not be an expression of the God-man relationship? So we believe. Yet how difficult to practice! We are caught up in the changes that have overtaken family life. Father, whether he likes it or not, is no longer the autocrat that Clarence Day knew. Mother is no longer so tied to the household chores that she lacks time for other interests. Where is the child who is seen and not heard? Perplexity and confusion are the result in many homes. The Church must help in establishing a new understanding of Christian family life.

All this and more we seek to teach. In whatever work we undertake to do, let us be sure of our objectives. The basketball coach can ask himself, as surely as can the youth counselor, what profit is there in winning the game, holding the meeting, or teaching the class, if these youth do not learn to love God and to love their neighbor? All that we do is surrounded with others. Our dual goal is to help persons grow and develop in relationship to God and to their fellow man. All that has been learned about the operation of groups and the effect of persons on each other is needed if we are to accomplish this goal.

Learning

The teacher of a leadership class said to her students, "What are you teaching?"

"I'm teaching this first unit in the quarterly," said one.

"I'm teaching the Bible," was the firm response of another.

"I'm doing a unit on social problems," answered a third.

A young teacher looked up thoughtfully and ventured, "I am trying to teach children."

We have our purposes. We have our material. And always we are working with people, trying to help them to learn and grow. From time to time we must re-examine our objectives to be sure we are heading in the right direction—toward the highest goal. So must we also rethink our understanding of how people learn. We know today that a teacher cannot pour knowledge from her own wisdom into the heads of her students. She is a guide, a helper. She points the path or opens the door. She may stimulate, prod, or encourage, but learning can only be done by the learner himself.

Ask a class of adults to think of something they have learned recently. Invariably faces go blank. There is an amused though embarrassed silence. Then each begins to search himself: "When did I last learn something?"

A woman says she learned a new recipe from a television

33

program, but she cannot tell us the ingredients. A salesman in the group says he learned a new and better route for reaching a certain customer, and he tells us exactly how to follow it. Which of these two has learned? When can we say that learning has taken place?

Suppose you wanted to learn to swim. You read a book which describes the process. You study the pictures. You listen to someone telling how to swim. Perhaps you watch a movie in which an expert swims beautifully. You even practice the strokes sprawled across a stool in your living room. Have you learned to swim? Not until you get in the water, accept its buoyancy in faith, and try your strokes with some success, can you be said to have learned to swim.

Or take learning to drive a car. No driver-education program is complete without a car. The learner may study and practice in a classroom situation, but until he gets behind the wheel and begins to put the ideas into practice, he does not learn to drive. And it is not until the actions are almost automatic that we say, "This man has learned how to drive."

The story is told of an old Chinese farmer who came to the mission to learn Christianity. In the due course of his studies he was given the Beatitudes to memorize. For a long time he struggled, unable to commit the passage to memory. Then one morning after a long absence he appeared at school, his face bright with a smile.

"I have it! I have it!" he exclaimed, and repeated the passage perfectly.

The missionary was delighted and praised the old man. Then he said, "Farmer, you had so much trouble memorizing. How did you finally do it?"

The answer came quietly, humbly, "Pastor, I took each one

by itself and tried it out. When I found that they worked, I had them by heart."

Consider all the skills and understandings which an infant has learned by the time he is a year old. He has learned how to propel himself, how to get what he wants in one way or another. He has learned to distinguish the people in his household. He knows what to expect in the daily routine. He has strong likes and dislikes and ways of showing these feelings.

How did he learn all he knows? Did someone stand before him and teach him? Did someone read a lesson to him? Of course not! The idea is ridiculous.

Many of our learnings—certainly most of our earliest learnings—come through association with the people among whom we live. We learn by being a part of our surroundings. The pattern and the routine—both of thought and of action —flow around us, and most of us fall in line. The accepted practices, the family customs, the attitudes and habits become our own as we live within them.

Many times we learn through unplanned experiences and accidents. After cracking our heads several times, we learn to shut the doors of overhead cabinets. When we have tripped again and again over an uneven crack in the front sidewalk, we learn to avoid it. The young child speaks trustingly to everyone he meets on the street. He learns from the impatient look, the annoyed response, the cold shoulder, that all people are not equally friendly.

In his earliest experiences of visiting the church, the child begins to form unconsciously his understanding of what church is, whether or not it is a friendly place, and what his part in it will be. Let us not minimize the importance of these earliest learnings. We know how difficult it is to change our own, or another's, first bad impressions.

35

Mother takes the baby with her when she goes to a church meeting. Sunlight through the colored windows, throwing color on the floor, delights the infant. Stretching his fingers toward the dancing hues, he coos his pleasure. Perhaps a neighbor who plays with him often smiles at him in this strange building. He hears music, his mother and all the other people singing. Perhaps there are even refreshments and a bit of cake for the baby.

What has he learned? Nothing in words. But do you not see him beginning at least to love the church? And would not the opposite be equally true if his first experiences were unpleasant?

Your child gets angry and spits out a stream of oaths one day. You are shocked. Where did he learn such language? No one taught him. He heard the strange words used by another child and noted the effect their use had on his companions. He tried them himself and was proud of his accomplishment. Now he notes your dismay or irritation. He will probably use them again when he feels the need to disturb you. Learning occurs in many devious ways.

Much of our learning, however, is the result of planned guidance and direction. We are taught in practical situations how to eat at the table, how to meet people, how to cross the street safely, how to tie our shoestrings. Our parents and our teachers, by their example and their inducements, try to teach us the things which they think it is important for us to learn.

Motives

But consider this: Their success in teaching depends almost entirely on their ability to arouse in us, by one means or another, the desire and the effort to learn.

36

Take for example the mother who despairs of ever teaching her adolescent son to wash his hands, comb his hair, and dress neatly.

"Aw, what's the use? You just get messed up again as soon as you go out." He can see no reason for doing what she wishes, except to keep her from nagging him.

But one morning he comes to breakfast in a clean shirt, necktie, hands scrubbed, and even some vaseline on his hair. He has found a reason for learning how to dress well.

And so the matter of how learning takes place becomes not so much a question of how as why. The salesman learns a new route because it is more efficient. The child learns to swear because he likes the novelty and the effect. The boy learns to dress neatly because he wants a girl to like him. If the teacher can arouse sufficient interest and desire to learn, the battle is more than half won. When the learner's motive is strong, he will take the lead. The teacher becomes a guide and a resource, sometimes a restraining influence, but more often an opener of doors.

What are the motives that compel people to learn? At first glance they all seem to be selfish. Perhaps not. Let us think about them.

To please others is one of our first motives for learning. We want others to like us. We want their good will, their admiration, their respect. It may be that we want to please them simply because we love them with no thought for ourselves. Usually, however, when we struggle to learn how to dress, how to eat properly, how to conduct ourselves socially, or because of someone we love or admire, it is with the hope of receiving a word of praise or some sign of affection.

To a growing youngster it is all important to belong to the gang. He will do anything, learn anything, in order to be

37

accepted. In one gang baseball may be the focal point. So Billy practices pitching and catching, pitching and catching, hour after hour. In another gang adeptness at stealing may be the mark of distinction. So Joe patiently and doggedly learns the tricks of the trade.

We learn some things in order to prevent unpleasant experiences. If Johnny fails in arithmetic, the home atmosphere will be most unpleasant. So he struggles to learn enough of the subject to get a passing grade, though the whole thing may be extremely distasteful to him.

Sometimes we learn because we see pleasure in the results just for ourselves. The old lady who takes up painting at the age of seventy, and the young mother who takes up sculpture as a hobby, probably have no other motive than enjoyment. Bill learns to sail a boat, Joan learns to ride a horse, Peggy learns a difficult piece on the piano—each has primarily the motive of contributing to his own enjoyment.

To get something is the motive for much of our learning: to get a job, to get a reward, to get power or recognition, even to get praise.

And we learn in difficult situations where we have to solve a problem or meet a need. From the relatively simple matter of learning to operate a new type of stove to the terribly complex matter of learning to solve international problems, our lives are beset with situations where new learning is required.

We also have the desire to increase our knowledge of things which interest us and seem important to us. We go to lectures, read books, talk with people, because of our desire to know more about a subject that is fascinating to us.

Sometimes we learn because we want our lives to be useful. Red Cross courses and hospital-training programs for volunteers attract many through this motive. Men and women re-

38

spond to the call of youth agencies and the Church because they want to make some worth-while contribution to life. They give time, energy, and talent to learning the techniques of leadership. Boys and girls also respond in our programs because they want to help others.

No, the motives are not all selfish. And yet the motives are usually mixed. If Bill learns to sail, his friends will admire him and go with him. If we learn our hobby well, we get praise from our friends and may even find some financial reward in what we do. We learn in order to be useful, but we are not unaware that service and leadership bring other rewards in the forms of recognition, comradeship, and pleasure.

There is another aspect to this matter. Sometimes we, as leaders, have one motive, while our group is moved by a different motive. The coach of the church basketball team may want his boys to learn how to work together, how to be thoughtful of the other fellow. The team may want primarily to win. Or the teacher of junior-highs may want his class to share some important ideas with the department while their motive in the same program may be to win admiration. Such confusion of motives is rarely successful.

There comes a time in our Christian growth when we find the higher motive. Look at Albert Schweitzer. Why did he turn from a successful and worth-while career in philosophy and music to learn medicine? Or Kagawa. Why did he choose to learn about life in the slums?

Seeking this higher motive, we search the life and the mind of Jesus, not debating theological issues but eager in our human frailty to find his purposes and make them our own. We see in him one dominant goal—to win men to the Father. No other consideration stands out in his life as this does. The record tells of the boy listening and asking questions of the learned men in the temple. It shows us with what understanding he took hold of scripture. It gives us that strange account of temptation in the desert when lesser goals were offered and rejected.

Throughout the record we see that Jesus knew himself to belong to God. "Wist ye not that I must be about my Father's business?" (Luke 2:49.) "I came . . . to do . . . the will of him that sent me." (John 6:38.) "I am in the Father, and the Father in me." (John 14:10.) With that sense of belonging to the Father he found, in doing God's will, all the joys and satisfactions which we seek, often so unsuccessfully, in lesser motives.

The motives, then, for learning and for service in the Christian life are to serve and to please God, to find fellowship with him, to share in the work of Christ, to draw all men into the kingdom of God.

We have spoken of the objectives which we have for the groups with whom we work, what we would have them learn, how we would help them grow. Now we have spoken of how learning takes place and of the motives within the learner.

As we approach our work, whether it be teaching or leading in some other capacity, we must see clearly the objectives toward which we work. Then we must put ourselves into the mind of the learner, asking what motive can he have, what motive can I appeal to that will make him grasp this knowledge, this technique, this idea.

Think of Mrs. Russell, whom we visited in the primary department in Chapter One. Her objective in the unit of work on the church was to help her boys and girls grow in their understanding of the church and in their loyalty to it. Writing the letter was an activity which would prepare the boys and girls for a meaningful visit. Visiting the minister was an activity which would contribute to the achievement of the goal.

What motives could she depend on to make the boys and girls want to learn the information and the ideas in this unit? They would want her recognition and praise. They would find pleasure in talking with an important person. Writing a good letter would give them a sense of achievement or power. They had had enough good experiences with the church and the minister to want to find out more. Looking for the children's motives, Mrs. Russell saw the unit through their eyes. She gained a new point of view. She saw the persons whom she was trying to help, their needs and interests. The material became a tool, not an end in itself. The learning became an adventure in which she walked and searched with her boys and girls.

Groups

One thing remains to be said about our approach to our work. We live in groups, in a democracy. The family, the Sunday-school class, the gang, the club, the team, the youth fellowship, the woman's society, the official board—the list of all our groups would cover pages! All except the hermits have a need to belong. There are those who argue that we have made ourselves so dependent on groups that we are afraid to stand alone. And they speak much truth! Joe knew that stealing was wrong, yet he learned to steal in order to be accepted by the group.

Too much we follow the crowd. We accept the patterns and prejudices of those to whom we would belong. The high-school crowd adopts a common mode of dress, and pity the poor fellow whose family can't or won't supply him with the current fashion! Even as adults we want to know what the others are wearing when we go to a social function. We do not want to be conspicuous. Groups can be demanding, cruel, destructive.

There is, fortunately, another side to the picture, and most of us recognize it. While great men and women stand out as individuals and leaders in the forward march of mankind, they could never have achieved and consolidated their victories alone. George Washington may be called the father of our country, but if we follow the analogy out we will see that he had a "family" with him and behind him. As the minds of men worked together over the ideals of liberty and representative government, the new republic grew. All over the country groups—large and small, official and private— discussed, rejected, revised, and finally accepted the daring foundation on which the United States of America was laid.

History tells us Abraham Lincoln freed the slaves. But this is no more true than that you and I freed the slaves! The president was a leader in the emancipation movement. His hand held the pen and signed the proclamation. But again it was the minds of men, wrestling with the problems involved, finding solutions, and committing themselves to action that freed the slaves.

Every social movement that has bettered the life of man has been just that—a social movement involving the thought and will and action of many people. Pioneers point the way. A prophet cries in the wilderness. One may die for the cause. But not until enough of the people have changed their pattern of thinking can the new ideas flourish.

There is power and wisdom in the group above and beyond that which the individual may attain. Perhaps Jesus had this in mind when he said that two or three gathered together

42

could find his spirit. A group studying a problem sees it from many angles. A group founding a country brings to bear on that enterprise the best thought of the keenest minds.

This is not to say that thinking alone produces poor results. Far from it! The greatest plan may start in the mind of one man. He may even bring his idea to a high state of perfection by himself. But a George Washington or a Thomas Jefferson alone could never have achieved what the band of patriots wrought. Even Jesus—perhaps we should say especially Jesus—turned his plan over to a group to think through, make their own, and carry out.

In a democracy it is the right of every man to think and to express his own thoughts. It is also the responsibility of every man to share in the decisions of his country. Our schools today teach children to think, to reason together. When a student makes a statement, others may ask, "What is your reference? Where is your proof?" Boys and girls are taught how to find facts, how to evaluate what they read, how to report, how to lead a discussion, how to work in committees, how to put plans into effective action. Education today is an active learning process. Even primary children have gained some of the techniques of group procedure. And many a boy and girl, like Bob in Chapter One can lead a group into fruitful thinking and planning.

Leaders of groups have learned many principles and methods by which their work can become more effective and satisfying. We need to understand group composition and relationships, how to guide thinking and planning, how to lead discussions, and how to help the group evaluate.

You are the leader of a group! Do you see the tremendous opportunity that is yours? Yours it is to release the power of thought and expression. Yours it is to help men and women, boys and girls, to think creatively, to work at problems together. Through the "fellowship of kindred minds" you can help a group to rise to new levels of understanding and action.

What, then, is a group? How can you develop the skills and techniques of effective group leadership? The succeeding chapters endeavor to help you at these points.

CHAPTER III

WHAT IS A GROUP?

IT TAKES MORE THAN A COLLECTION OF INDIVIDUALS TO MAKE a group. The title of this chapter might well have been, "Take this Class," with the subtitle, "and make of it a group."

A Collection of Individuals

Here is a class of eight junior boys and girls starting a new church-school year in October. Most of them have been in the same class before. Several are new. All do not go to the same school. They live in different neighborhoods. There are several close friendships in the class. They have a new teacher, Miss Brown, who has little or no acquaintance with them.

On the surface we see an attractive young teacher in a smart tweed suit and matching hat. We see curly-headed Paul with flashing black eyes and ready grin. Next to him is little Bobby, who hates to be kidded about his size and who speaks gruffly to make up in voice what he lacks in height. Then there is Barbara, primly dressed in blue silk with a new blue hat and white gloves on her hands. Barbara's friend, Jean, sits close to her and whispers in her ear from time to time. Alice sits next to them, but apart from them. She is dressed in a simple cotton plaid. Straight bangs give a wide look to her rather serious face. She is a newcomer to the group. Completing the circle are three very wigglesome chums—Tommy, Joe,

45

and Phil. They delight in taking something from anyone nearby and then making it disappear by passing it invisibly from one to the other, all the while making a great pretense of innocence. Right now all eight are on their good behavior, waiting a chance to test out their new teacher.

Here is a collection of nine individuals. What might we see if we could read their thoughts at the beginning of this first Sunday together? Perhaps something like this:

Paul: "Gee, Miss Brown is pretty. I hope she's as nice as Miss Roberts."

Bobby: "I'm glad we have more boys than girls. I hope we get a chance to do things and not just answer questions."

Barbara: "I hope Miss Brown can make these boys behave. I like the way her hat matches her suit. I wonder if she prepares a lesson?"

Jean: "I wish I had white gloves like Barbara's. I wonder if Mother would buy me a pair?"

Alice: "I don't see why I had to come to Sunday school. Just because Mother thinks it's good for me. She and Daddy don't come. I don't know these kids. Not a one of them has spoken to me. Well, I'll just keep my mouth shut and think about the movie I saw yesterday."

Tommy: "Wonder how much we can get away with in this class? Anyway, Miss Brown doesn't look hardboiled."

Joe: "I bet we can get Bobby's goat without much trouble. Might as well have some fun in Sunday school."

Phil: "I wonder what this class is going to be like? Miss Brown looks okay. I could go along with her if she'd only let us do something interesting."

Miss Brown: "I'm scared to death! If only I can make these children like me. Please, Lord, help me make the first session a good one."

Here is a potential group, a collection of nine individuals who will meet regularly for the next twelve months. So far there is not one single interest shared by them all.

A Functioning Group

Here is a young parents' group on the same Sunday morning, buzzing with activity before the session formally begins. There is much talking and moving about. A newcomer is introduced to a young mother who immediately takes the initiative in getting further acquainted. Several committee chairmen use this time to get help on projects which the group has under way. Conversation can be overheard about children, school, sickness, absence of some regular members, jobs, shopping politics, books. When the chairman calls the group together, there is no hanging back. And there is no letup in conversation, only an enlargement into one conversation which includes the whole group. The topic is one previously chosen by the group. Interest is high. It is clear that some preparation has gone into this discussion. Reading is referred to for the purpose of illustrating or enforcing some point. There is a sense that these people are trying to understand each other, trying to learn from and with each other. What they are doing has importance for them. They participate actively.

As we note the difference between the individuals just beginning a group experience and the young adults whose interest is so keen, we can see some of the marks which distinguish the effective group in Christian education.

1. *Uniting of Minds*

The characteristic which stands out most as we look at the young adults is one of common interests and shared purposes in which they find a uniting of minds. Their common interests are many, ranging from family and jobs to books and politics. They speak a common language along many lines. This is not to say that they agree on everything. One mother rears her child "by the book" while another may go almost to the extreme of a "hands-off" policy. But both are concerned about their children and eager to do a good job with them. Employment in the group is diversified. There are chemists, clerks, teachers, farmers, businessmen, a lawyer, and a mechanic. True, most of them are in white-collar jobs or the professions, but there is a wide range of vocational activity. In educational background the members range from those who stopped at the end of high school to those who have advanced professional training. But all are concerned about the schooling their children shall receive. They do not agree on school policies, but they will discuss the schools at every opportunity. So it goes through a wide range of interests, not agreement, but a common concern. As they move into the morning's discussion, each brings his mind to bear on the problem at hand.

2. *Desire to Grow*

If we ask why these people have made the effort to come to the church school on a Sunday morning, we will see a second distinguishing characteristic of the effective group. It is significant that they have not "sent" their children or dropped them off at the door. The parents also have come because of their desire to grow. Their concern with the problems at hand, the reading they have done, their intent listening to others in the group—all indicate this.

Perhaps they acknowledge that the problems of rearing a family are too difficult in changing times. They need to compare notes with other parents, to get help. Perhaps they feel frustration in the face of politics and the desire for good government. Perhaps it is the questions children ask, and which parents echo, that bring them together—questions about God, life and death, prayer, and the Bible. These young adults have come together feeling a need and desiring to meet that need.

3. Shared Planning

Had we listened closely to the conversations at the beginning of the morning, we would have heard many people sharing in the planning for the activities of this group. There are chairmen for the several committees, there is a discussion leader, there is a secretary-treasurer who keeps the records, and a president. These leaders have learned that their function is not one of running the group, but rather of drawing the whole group into the planning and work of their many activities. It is their philosophy that everyone is important in formulating and carrying out the projects.

4. Group Decision

One of the things this group has learned to do well is to come to decisions together. The decision for action remains with the group. On some matters they agree to abide by a majority vote, but there are other matters on which no action is taken until there is common agreement. When a problem arises for decision, they look at it as a problem which we all must help to solve. They have learned to look for the best decision and to seek in another's thoughts and in the sharing of their own a better decision than anyone could make alone.

49

They have thought about the techniques of reaching decisions, and through much practice they have learned when a discussion must be halted to wait for new information and insight. On simpler problems they have learned how to move easily to the place of group agreement.

5. Concern for Each Individual

Another notable characteristic of this group is its concern for each individual. It is not just politeness that brings inquiries about health and children. The inquiries go deeper. They sometimes refer back to statements made earlier when a member was grappling with an idea. A member who is known to have difficulty expressing himself is helped by the leader and by the group members too. Through thinking and working together, they have developed a genuine interest in one another and a desire to help as well as to be helped.

6. Regularity

There is a certain group stability in meeting regularly and in having clearly defined functions. This group has developed a pattern of meeting and acting which is not stereotyped, but which leads to an expectancy and produces results. The place and time of meeting are consistent. There are also one or two stated times for sociability each month. There are committees for calling on newcomers, helping the sick, distributing literature, and for keeping the needs of church or community before the group. The members are therefore part of an ongoing stream which keeps them in active fellowship.

7. Action and Growth

The old maxim, "Nothing succeeds like success," applies to this group also. Growth through thought, reading, and discussion keeps the members coming back for more. Significant action gives them a sense of accomplishment. The value of being part of the group is brought home to them as they see their lives enriched by the contact. They decorated the sanctuary for Christmas, and the results brought pleasure. They grappled with local political problems and found an increased sense of competence in understanding them and dealing with them. They studied ideas of God in the Bible and grew in their realization of God's presence and meaning for themselves. Evaluation of themselves and of their functioning as a group is a regular activity. The conclusion of a unit of study or a project is followed by keen searching. They want to grow as individuals, but they also want to improve their techniques and effectiveness as a group.

8. Leading on

All problems are not solved by this group and all action does not result in completion. They have learned, however, the way to point their thinking toward the future. When in discussion they strike a tangent that cannot be solved at the time, they set it down for later consideration. Action which meets stone walls of indifference or currently insurmountable difficulties is laid aside temporarily but not forgotten. When new facts, new leads, new personalities are found, the problem is attacked again. Often one interest leads to another. As one study is brought to a conclusion, another opens up. The study of biblical ideas of God led to a study of other religions and a new affirmation of Christianity. Each study of children and the family leads them on to a new area of thought. The group is characterized by a sense of value in what they do and a desire to go on. New members are welcomed as an opportunity to bring new thinking and new personalities to the group. Positions of leadership are changed often, not only to keep the group from growing stale, but because the group is always looking for new talent and new enthusiasm. They resist the temptation to glory in past accomplishments or to say "Let's do it the way we did last year." They look from the present to the future. They are alert and eager to move forward.

Back to Miss Brown

The problem Miss Brown faces at the start of the new year with a new class is how to lead the juniors toward effective group functioning. Assuming that she desires to accomplish the purposes set forth in Chapter Two, and that she believes that education must involve the mental activity of the pupil and the interaction of the group, let us see what steps she must take.

How would the eight characteristics of an effective group apply to the collection of individuals which she faces? At this point almost every criteria must be answered in the negative. There is no uniting of minds around a common interest. The desire to grow is not evident. So far there has been no opportunity for planning or decision. Little concern for each other is shown by the individuals in the group. They do have a regular time of meeting. They have not had the satisfaction of fruitful action and growth. They have as yet no background from which to lead on.

Develop Fellowship

The criteria, however, can indicate the starting place for Miss Brown and her group. The emphasis has shifted from "How shall I teach this lesson?" to "How shall I help these children?" This does not mean that the lesson material is put aside. Rather it is put in a new perspective. Its reason for existence is to help these children grow. And so Miss Brown must give first consideration to the children. Who are they? Who are their families and what are their homes like? What do they enjoy? What abilities do they have? What are their needs? How can I get to know them? How can I build friendliness among them and between them and me so that we shall want to be together?

So the first session is spent, with some laughter and fun, in getting acquainted and in talking over likes and dislikes. The leader must have a genuine interest in the boys and girls as persons. She must let them get to know her likes and dislikes and something of her family and friends. The boys and girls must be the center of interest, however. It is a time for developing fellowship and friendliness, an acknowledgment of the fact that we are set together for this church-school year.

The next step is the development of a common interest. In some groups this may be achieved through the simple means of planning a picnic or hike. Others may want to take a trip to some place of interest, or begin to make something, start a hobby, or work on some project.

Set Goals

Very soon after the first meeting, or possibly at the first meeting, the group should set up some goals for itself for the coming year. In Miss Brown's class these may be: (a) to do something interesting; (b) to learn about the Bible; (c) to help with the work of the church; (d) to have good times together. From time to time they will want to look at these goals, revise them, and add new ones. A recreational group planning to meet regularly through the year might list their goals as: (a) to improve our skill; (b) to develop good team-work; (c) to test our playing, our fun, and our friendships by our Christian beliefs. A group united for the purpose of producing plays might say that they want: (a) to make money for the church; (b) to learn techniques of acting and stage production; (c) to entertain. Another group united by the same skill interest but different motives might list as their goals: (a) to study church drama; (b) to produce plays that will challenge people's thinking or lead them in worship; (c) to increase our ability as actors or technicians.

The statement of goals becomes a guide by which the group can check and evaluate itself as time passes. It must be the sincere expression of the group. How foolish for the first drama group above to list the purposes of the second! If their interest at the start is primarily to make money, let them say so. Later they may revise their goals to add another. But to start off with a false statement of goals is like saying, "I'm going to California," and then starting off in the opposite direction.

In a class situation it is particularly important that the teacher help the pupils to make an honest statement of purpose. By experience the pupils may assume that the teacher wants them to list goals acceptable to her. Or they may hope to win her favor by listing the goals which they think she wants. The junior class listing the goals above may have put in the second and third goals—about the Bible and the church—only because they thought it was expected. A wise teacher who has faith in her boys and girls will hold them to a statement of goals which they honestly mean at this point, knowing that other higher goals will come later when the group is under way.

The seeds of friendliness are sown, and a statement of purposes is made. What comes next if this class is to grow into an effective group? Planning comes next; planning toward the goals. How shall we accomplish what we want to do?

Planning

Here we might recall three of the guide questions which we used as we visited the church school in Chapter One. What evidence is there that the pupils are mentally active? Are the pupils following directions, or are they sharing actively in the planning and the work? How much responsibility are the pupils taking?

Having launched into the experience of proceeding on group principles, the teacher or leader must follow through. The pupils must have their rightful share in the planning. It is important to note, however, that younger groups need to learn how to plan, need to grow by small experiences to be ready for larger ones. In the nursery department we visited the children did no planning at all, but they did share the responsibility of putting toys away. Remember also that when Chris hit Jimmy, the teachers held back. The physical hurt was not tragic, and they felt it important to wait before stepping in to let the children take care of the problem by themselves as far as possible. The kindergarten children had not planned the session, but they did plan their dramatization of the story. On the other hand, in the junior-high group a ninth-grader was taking the lead in attacking a problem, and his fellow students faced it with him. The process of growing up is one of achieving more and more self-control and self-direction. The problem for parents and teachers is to know how much responsibility the child is ready for. To give him too little will cause dissatisfaction. To expect him to take more responsibility than he is ready for will usually result in failure.

So planning is a problem, particularly with children's groups. For example, suppose Miss Brown's group had listed only two goals: (a) to do something interesting; (b) to have fun. They are a church-school class, and as such it is expected that they will make use of the lesson materials. The problems of a completely unplanned curriculum more than outweigh its opportunities in most church schools. Therefore we follow a set of lesson materials, hoping that through the process our children will gain some knowledge and insight on the Bible, the Church, and the religious life. Miss Brown has the responsibility now of putting the lesson materials within the framework of the children's goals.

She may say, "This is our lesson material for the year. How can we use it in such a way that we will do interesting things and have fun?" From that point the juniors can enter into the planning of how the material can be used and the goals reached. The teacher has stated the obvious limits within which they must work.

How different if she had said, "Well, all right, we'll take a trip or have a party, but first we have to study our lesson!"

Action

We begin to build a good group through friendliness, through setting goals, and planning. Then comes action, and in most cases the sooner the better! The juniors planned how to make the study of Joseph interesting. They decided to make a series of dioramas, or small stage sets, to show the various scenes of the story. What came first? They had to find out what was in the story, of course. They attacked the lesson materials eagerly—to find out something which they wanted to know. They went after other materials to find out what houses, landscapes, and costumes looked like at that time.

56

They took responsibility for getting the boxes, cloth, paper, and paint. In the four weeks allotted to the story, Joseph came alive. The juniors got information, they used it to make the dioramas, and they shared with the department what they had learned and made.

Evaluation

We follow up action with evaluation if we want to grow in our group life. These juniors asked all sorts of questions at the end of their unit on Joseph. Some were questions about what they had learned in point of fact. Other questions had to do with how we worked as a group. Did everybody do his part? Did we help each other, or did someone just work by himself? When we had discussions, did we stick to the point, and did everybody share his thinking? The teacher asked questions too. Did I give you enough help? Did I do too much? Did I listen with equal interest to everybody's ideas? Did we all give recognition and praise where it was due? Some questions were suggested for each individual to ask himself. Did I do my share? Could the group depend on me when I said I would do something? Which session did I enjoy most? Why? Which session did I enjoy least? Why? What new thing did I find out about someone in the group?

If we could listen in to the thoughts of Miss Brown's juniors after the experience with Joseph, how differently they would sound! They are happy to be together and are on their way to a good church-school year. Within the limits of their experience they are already a good group.

Does it sound easy to build this fellowship? Does the young-adult class pictured here seem too good to be true? There are such groups. And it is not too hard to build the group feeling.

There are techniques for studying and evaluating groups and there are skills needed for leadership. Chapter Four offers some suggestions to guide the leader in studying and developing his group. Subsequent chapters present some of the practical skills which the leader needs.

CHAPTER IV

SOME TECHNIQUES FOR STUDYING A GROUP

THE STUDY OF GROUPS IS ESSENTIALLY A STUDY OF INDIVIDUALS and their reactions to and their effect on other individuals. The reason for attempting to understand group relationships and activity more clearly is to help us do a better job in developing, freeing, and guiding each person in the group. When we study the individuals in our class or club and their group experiences, our goal is better leadership or better teaching because of our commitment to the purposes of Jesus.

Checkup on Individuals

The first essential is to learn to know well each individual in the group. Beyond knowing him as a person, if we are to understand him, we must know something of his background, his family, his interests or hobbies, his physical and mental abilities and limitations, and his economic problems—if any. All these are factors contributing to the individual's growth or lack of it, and to his participation in group life.

John was a poorly dressed boy by comparison with others in his class. He came to church school alone, and the other children in the class tended to ignore him. He usually needed a haircut and sometimes his neck and ears were noticeably dirty. As far as his teacher could judge, he paid little attention

59

in class. His comments were off the topic, and his foot-shuffling and poking the fellow next to him were an irritating distraction. His teacher found herself increasingly annoyed by the boy. When she realized that she had begun to hope he wouldn't come to church school, she knew she had to change her attitude or admit defeat as a church-school teacher. She began to collect all the information she could get about John.

She found that his parents were separated and both living elsewhere. John lived with an older married sister who had two small children of her own. Though he himself was only eleven, John was often pressed into service as a baby sitter. The home was crowded and badly in need of paint and repairs, yet the car in the drive was no more than a year old and the house contained such conveniences as a wide-screen television set, new washing machine, and a first-class refrigerator. A little conversation revealed that both the sister and her husband were employed. Their hours occasionally overlapped, and then John was responsible alone for the four-year-old and the seven-year-old. The house was rented and the car and utilities were being bought on installment.

One day the teacher asked John about his hobbies. Didn't he collect something?

John shrugged his shoulders. "What's the use? Where would I keep it? Those two kids never leave my stuff alone."

John's teacher found both her attitude and her relationship with the boy changing. By studying him, she had come to understand him a little better. With understanding came genuine caring. This was a good beginning. With it came a new relationship in the class—not quickly, but gradually.

Another teacher making a routine visit at the home of one of her pupils learned for the first time that the boy was an artist. The mother proudly brought out pieces of her son's work. A friendly relationship was strengthened by the teacher's interest and pleasure in the boy's work. From that time she noted that he became a more active participant in the class discussions and projects.

A guide for learning more about the pupils in one's class may be unnecessary in a few small churches where everybody knows everybody and no new families are moving in. In these days such churches are few and far between. The dispersal of industrial plants, the movement of city-employed people to live in the country, and the general mobility of America today provide nearly every church with the opportunity to welcome newcomers to its fellowship. That some people in some churches do not welcome newcomers is a sad fact. Such people are apparently not motivated by the objectives set forth in Chapter Two, and this book is probably not for them.

Wherever new people are coming into our classes and clubs, we can help them and ourselves to a better relationship by getting to know something more about them than their names and addresses. Writing down what information we have reveals more clearly what we do not know. Teachers of children and youth find it particularly helpful to make note of the kinds of information suggested on the "Guide for Getting Better Acquainted." This is information which will not and should not be gotten all at once. Most teachers get these facts through informal conversation with the pupil. More can be learned by listening to the child's conversation with his friends. Our understanding of a person is probably never complete, but a friendly visit to him at home helps more than anything else. The longer we know him, the more we learn about him. Most teachers who have tried it find that keeping a notebook or record in which entries are frequently made for each pupil helps them to add and keep many small bits of information which together indicate important needs, growth, or abilities. In such a record we note with date any unusual behavior, anything which is a departure from what would normally be expected. We jot down questions or comments which the person makes. Over a period of time we may find a common thread running through such comments which reveals a deep-seated need or problem. Such a record helps us to remember birthdays and to show keener interest in illnesses.

With adults the "Guide for Getting Better Acquainted" may well be a shared enterprise, with the responses open to everyone in the group. None of this information is confidential, none of it is opinion. In younger groups the teacher will know a great deal more about each pupil than the boys and girls are to know about each other. The teacher will see that interesting facts about hobbies and abilities find a way into the group discussion. She will be concerned to help her pupils get to know each other well, but much of the information which she gathers will be confidential in nature.

In an older group the teacher or leader is one of the group. In such experiences as we have described, the group has a sense of responsibility for itself. There is friendliness, mutual interest and concern, a meeting of kindred minds. Such a group is helped by greater knowledge of each other's interests, abilities, homes, work, and problems. A committee might be responsible for getting the information called for on the guide, or a session might be spent on getting better acquainted. In this session each person might fill in his own information sheet. After some small group discussions volunteers might be asked to tell some interesting fact they have just learned about someone else. Some fellowship singing, a game or two, and refreshments would make a pleasant evening when the friendliness within the group would be greatly strengthened.

The two following guide sheets are suggestive of (a) the type of information which will be helpful to the leader of young people and children; (b) the kinds of information which help adult groups to know each other better.

A Guide for Getting Better Acquainted with Children and Youth

NAME:

CHILD IS LIVING WITH:
both parents _____
one parent _____
relatives _____
in foster home _____
in orphanage _____
adopted _____

APPARENT ECONOMIC STATUS: Much above Average for Much below
average community average

APPEARANCE OF HOME: Much above Average for Much below
average community average

SCHOOL GRADE: _____(date)

AGE: _____(year, month, and day of birth)

DESCRIBE PHYSICAL STATURE AND CHARACTERISTICS BRIEFLY:

NAMES AND AGES OF BROTHERS IN HOME:

_____ _____ _____

NAMES AND AGES OF SISTERS IN HOME:

_____ _____ _____

OTHER PERTINENT INFORMATION: (add to this as you learn)

HOBBIES:

SHOWS INTEREST IN:

IS ACTIVE IN:

TALENTS AND SPECIAL ABILITIES:

63

A Guide for Getting Better Acquainted with Adults

NAME: BIRTHDAY:

DESCRIBE PHYSICAL STATURE AND CHARACTERISTICS BRIEFLY:

HOME SITUATION: lives alone   _____
                   lives with friends_____
                   lives with relatives
                   (indicate relationship)
                                          _____

                   lives with husband
                     (or wife)   _____
                   names and birth dates of
                     children (or grand-
                     children)   _____

EMPLOYMENT: where and type work
                                          _____
                   is husband (or wife) also
                     employed:
                   where and what:
                   Retired:_____ When:_____

EDUCATION: High school_____ College _____
                   Major field _____ Graduate study _____

PARTICIPATION IN OTHER ACTIVITIES: (such as clubs, fraternal orders,
   scouting, etc.)

INTERESTS AND HOBBIES:

SPECIAL ABILITIES:

SPECIAL PROBLEMS: (such as illness in home, poor health, dis-
   abilities, etc.)

Checkup on Reactions

In most groups there are likely to be some antagonisms and
some close friendships. If we study the reactions of the various

members to each other, we get a better clue as to needs and problems. We also push ourselves to look and listen more closely to the quiet person who gives little reaction at all. Such a person sometimes needs help in feeling secure and free to express himself. He may simply need the reassurance of more friendly interest. Or his problems may be so great that he retreats into a quiet world of the mind—all of his own making—and refuses to participate in the real world. At least through noting reactions, the leader becomes a little more conscious of each person in the group.

A copy of a reaction chart which might be used over a period of weeks is included here. Even six sessions are enough in which to develop a keener awareness of each person's relationship to the others in the group.

The chart is meant for the teacher's or leader's private use as he thinks back over the session fairly soon after the group leaves. Since doing the chart in private demands dependence on memory, most leaders make a time for it on the same day or evening of the group meeting.

If the group is large, it is not feasible to attempt to chart the antagonisms and interests of everyone in it. Five or six persons are probably as many as one leader can study in this manner at one time. It is suggested for larger groups that assisting teachers help with the study, or that the teacher study a few individuals for six weeks and then shift to a few others. At the start the leader may profit by studying just one individual for several weeks until he feels at ease with the technique. Where two leaders work together in a group, the situation is excellent for one to make notes on the chart while the other is taking responsibility for the discussion. In this situation a number of group members can easily be observed at the same time.

This charting of interests and antagonisms is, of course, usable only where there is some freedom within the group. The teacher needs to be present early since some of the frankest interchange will take place as the group gathers. The teacher will note who comes with whom, who is in which conversation group, who tries to edge in, and who sits with whom. If the group situation is such that the members are expected to sit still and keep quiet for the duration of the session, the leader will note very little interaction. He will be limited to an observation of who comes and leaves with whom. This study should show for one thing whether there is sufficient opportunity for interaction and response in the group session.

The chart calls for an indication of three types of interest and three types of antagonism. These qualities may be exhibited in many different ways. The older the group the more subtle the form of antagonism usually becomes. A term of endearment used very cattily is a form of attacking. Four-year-olds would use a more exact word, but their meaning would be no more clearly understood.

Three words have been selected to indicate three different ways in which a person may show interest. The three words need rather wide interpretation. "Choosing" may imply choosing to sit beside the person. Or it may mean choosing to say something to that person. It may mean selecting the person to serve on a committee. There is no particular need to indicate on the form the kind of choosing. Over the six weeks a pattern of choosing may or may not show itself.

Showing interest by "interrogating" may mean that Alice asks Jean about last night's party or tomorrow's plans. It may mean that Bill asks David for the answer to a problem. Perhaps George asks Mary Ann what she thinks about something. It is simply an indication that the one person turns to the other with an inquiry.

To show interest by "following" would indicate that the one chosen or spoken to returned the interest although he had not taken the initiative. Joe says, "Sit here," and George promptly sits. Sally asks Mary Ann about last night's date, and the latter responds. Bill accepts being chosen for the committee or job. Sally falls in line with Jean's suggestion.

Antagonisms are of particular interest to the leader who wants to help his group achieve the goal of loving our neighbor. Just as Jesus was not content with the outward expression but sought to reach the depths of human life, so the teacher or group leader needs to grow in his awareness of those inner antagonisms which negate Christian love.

Antagonism which is expressed by "attacking" is usually visible within the small group. At first the young child attacks physically, later with words after he has learned to substitute words for actions. Young people and adults are more likely to attack by words, or by joining forces with others who dislike a person, to put the person out. Attacking is a form of action which has as its objective the discomfort or the elimination of the one attacked.

If George refuses to sit by the one who asks him, he is showing antagonism by "rejecting" the person who asked him. We reject by refusing to co-operate, to sit, or to talk with a person who seeks us out. We sometimes reject by opposing another's idea in discussion. It is very difficult to oppose the idea without opposing the person. Children reject persons very readily and frankly. They say freely whom they do not want in the game or on the committee.

Less violent but still unloving is the antagonism which takes the form of "ignoring" a person. He is neither attacked nor positively rejected, hence the antagonist cannot be accused of any untoward action. It is most difficult for the leader to see and to reach this type of antagonism. The person who employs it does not hit, kick, or call names. If spoken to by the one disliked, he answers just enough to satisfy his feeling for being decent or polite, then turns away quickly.

Keeping this chart serves, first of all, the purpose of making the leader more generally aware of the feelings of the persons in his group. It helps him to develop sensitivity to those toward whom antagonism is shown. It puts him in a better position, because of his increased understanding, to help each person grow.

Here are directions for keeping the reaction chart.

1. On the top line write the name of the member to be observed. On the succeeding lines write the names of other members in the group. If the group is very large, write in the names of others only as this member reacts to them.

2. Each week mark I and A after the names of group members to whom this person reacted.

3. There may, of course, be more than one I or A each week. Do not let last week's I or A influence you. You may have been wrong last week. Also, relationships change.

KEY TO SYMBOLS:

I_1 : showed strong interest in by choosing
I_2 : showed strong interest in by interrogating
I_3 : showed strong interest in by following
A_1: expressed antagonism toward by attacking
A_2: expressed antagonism toward by opposing or rejecting
A_3: expressed antagonism toward by ignoring

68

NAME OF CHILD: Barbara	DATES				
CLASS MEMBERS	OCT. 4	OCT. 11	OCT. 18	OCT. 25	NOV. 1
Alice	A_3		A_2		A_2
Jean	$I_{1,2}$	I_1	$I_{1,3}$	$I_{1,2}$	I_1
Paul		I_2			
Bobby					
Tom	A_1		I_2	A_2	
Phil					

Note: In the example given, Barbara on October 4th has shown antagonism toward Tom by attacking him. She said to the teacher, "Tom is so dumb. Nobody likes him in school. He can't do anything right."

Barbara expressed antagonism toward Alice by politely ignoring her request to "Sit here, Babs." She gave no sign that she heard, though the request was clearly audible, and went across the circle to sit by Jean. She began immediately to ask Jean about some experience of the day before.

Over the weeks she consistently shows interest in Jean and antagonism toward Alice. She shows a one-session interest in Paul. Her antagonism toward Tom becomes interest in one session as she asks him something. The very next session she rejects him.

The leader may tentatively conclude that Barbara is a girl who needs some help in widening her circle of friends. She also apparently has some feeling against Alice and may need help to grow into a more friendly relationship there. Perhaps Alice needs further study to see what it is in her that causes Barbara's antagonism. Alice may need help. The leader may also want to study Jean's pattern of interactions. Is she almost exclusively interested in Barbara? Does she show the same antagonisms?

Checkup on Participation

Another type of check list which will help a leader observe more carefully the participation of the members of his group is shown in the table displayed on the next page. Here we learn more about a person by the way he contributes or withholds in the group. The boy who consistently says nothing is a boy in need of close study and help. Another who only answers questions is also in need of help. For some reason these boys are not at ease in the group. The wise leader seeks the reason first. When she knows that, then she is ready to help. A chart such as this one points up the need for better understanding.

On the positive side the chart is an indication not only of ability, but also of attitude. It will help a leader see when thinking has been going on in between sessions, as when a member brings in resource materials or links some other experience of his to what the group is discussing.

If the chart is kept for a month in the fall and again for a month in the spring, it should show some interesting growth. Does the boy who said nothing now share in the discussion? Do others, who never brought in materials or writing of their own, now do so? Have the negative checks decreased for everyone?

A Check on Participation in the Group

WAYS OF PARTICIPATION							
asks questions							
answers questions							
shares ideas							
makes suggestions							
shares information voluntarily from silent reading or study							
shares ideas for group writing							
does some creative writing alone and shares it							
readily takes role in dramatization							
shares a pertinent experience							
works well with hands							
shows art ability in drawing							
volunteers for clean-up job							
reminds others to clean up							
brings materials or resources to the group							
makes distracting comments							
says nothing							
forgets something he promised to do							
leaves job incomplete							
has to be reminded to put things away							

NAME OF MEMBER _____ DATES

When the record for everyone in the group is noted, the leader will have an indication of the extent to which participation is shared. Are the responses, the discussion, and the activity limited to a small minority? Has the leader been content to get the "right answers" and a creditably finished activity, no matter how few take part? In a sense the leader will perforce be evaluating himself and his objectives as a leader. Has this emphasis been on the finished product rather than on developing persons?

Checkup on Relationships

Any group that is larger than four in number may have smaller groupings within it. These may be friendship groups, school cliques, interest groups, or work committees. They may be planned or unplanned. The leader who would study his group needs to study the members as they participate in these subgroups. A social affair or an informal period before or after the group meeting is an excellent time to observe these more intimate interactions. The leader can also make provision for smaller groups within the class or meeting time.

When planning is done by a group, there are likely to be committees. These committees may work within the session or between sessions. Large groups need the smaller groupings in order to give every member a sense of belonging and responsibility. Sometimes these smaller groupings are planned, but more often they are the unplanned friendship groups. The same people will come with the same friends, sit together, generally think alike, and maintain loyalty to the larger group because of their belonging within the small group.

The leader who wishes to study his group and develop a keener understanding of it can profit by charting the subgroups within it from time to time. Are these natural or planned groups? How does the pattern change over a period of time? Do the planned groups have some effect on the natural groupings? For example, does the friendship pattern within a group change after the members have been working in committees not selected on a friendship basis? The leader will become conscious of the "natural" leaders in the small groups. Around whom do the friendships revolve? Whose standards have most effect on the group standards? Who are the high-prestige people? On what does prestige depend?

All of these questions will be in the mind of the alert leader as he quietly observes his group in action and as he later reflects upon their behavior.

He may jot down in his notebook rough notes such as the following: "Joe, Harry, and Mary Lou come in together. Sue, here alone, joins them. Mary Lou and Harry talking fast. Joe laughs. Sue tries to get word in, but mostly just agrees with what they say.

"Bill and Donald in together. Sit down on sidelines. Freddy joins them, but they ignore him. Freddy leaves. Freddy sits within range of first group and makes comments. No one takes notice.

"Henrietta, Jane, and Ruth come in, go toward browsing table. Add materials to it.

"George comes in alone. Freddy grabs him by arm. George pushes Freddy away and looks around. Sees everybody else occupied. Talks to Freddy. They go to browsing table. Girls leave. Mary Lou calls Bill. He and Donald join her group. The three girls also sit down nearby. Freddy and George go to other side of room."

Observing over a period of weeks and finding a somewhat similar pattern, what can the leader conclude? He has seen one girl and boy who have learned how to be at ease with each other. They have the friendly relationship which the others want. To have a boy friend or a girl friend gives high prestige to a young teen-ager. Mary Lou has that. She will have to be in on the planning of whatever this group does. If she is for it, most of the others will be too. The person she chooses, as when she singled out Bill and called him, also goes up in prestige.

But what about Freddy and George? How can they be helped to make a worth-while contribution? Left on the fringes, they are likely to create a disturbance in order to be noticed; or they may simply withdraw from the group. The leader who makes a practice of keeping notes on his group will see the danger signals and be looking for opportunities to draw these boys in.

Checkup on Discussion

In the chapter on discussion there is a diagram showing that discussion should go "this way, not this way." Discussion is so necessary to group planning and the exchange of ideas that it is very important for a leader and a group to check up occasionally on their use of this technique. One of the best ways in which to check up is to have an observer—a member of the group in older groups; a parent or assistant teacher in younger groups—diagram the discussion. To do this, he sketches in a seating arrangement showing where each person sits. During the discussion he draws a continuous line back and forth across the diagram from one speaker to the next. He must concentrate on who is speaking and not on what is said. When the exchange of comments is brief and quick, the observer may have difficulty keeping up. If he loses one speaker on the diagram, he must take up the next and quickly go on. He never interrupts the discussion. And he should be seated just outside the group where his activity will not be a distraction.

At the end of the discussion of the topic, time should be allotted for a study of the diagram. Some members have no idea of the amount of their participation. All will be interested to see themselves in relation to the others. If such diagrams are kept on file, a group may compare the current one with previous ones in an effort to see growth.

Growth must also be measured in terms of quality of contributions. Is the group making rich use of facts and resources? Is the discussion profitable? Does it lead toward action and growth? Discussion is so important to the life of a group that Chapter Five has been devoted to it.

Checkup on Growth

There come times in the life of a group, as in the life of an individual, when there is need to look backward in order to be sure that we are going forward. This process is known as evaluation.

One of the values in setting goals is that from time to time we can look at the goals and inquire into our progress toward them. Christian-education groups may have several different types of goals. The evaluation will always be in terms of the goal under consideration. An adult group may set goals for itself in terms of Bible knowledge, service activities, attendance, and enrollment. Each goal needs its own kind of checkup. If the group has also set as a goal the development of better group procedures and relationships, this calls for another type of evaluation.

Evaluation in this area must be in terms of quality and

quantity of participation, relationships of members, responsibility taken, types of leadership given, carry-over of ideas into daily living, and deepened conviction of the value of the group for Christian witness, study, planning, and action. Church groups will also want to study both the group's and the individual's relationship to other groups, to the whole church, and to the community. Outreach is one of the marks of the Christian group, concern not just for itself and its own members, but concern for its share in the wider fellowship.

There are numerous techniques for evaluating the group process and life. One is the discussion diagram just described. Another is the quick end-of-meeting evaluation. In this each member at the last minute rates the session from 1 to 5 on a little piece of paper, and leaves the paper with a recorder. If the member feels the group has had a very excellent session with good participation, thinking, and accomplishment, he will put the number 1 on his paper. If he feels that this was the worst possible session, with ragged discussion and time wasted, he will write down 5. The numbers 2, 3, and 4 represent a scale of opinion from 1 to 5. The recorder compiles the results and announces it to the group at the next session. Before discussion on the topic for the day begins, the leader may ask for some illumination from the members as to why they felt the previous session was good or bad and what can be done to improve it.

A technique used by larger groups is evaluation by a committee which reports its findings and recommendations. The committee may interview members, make a survey, make note of the discussions and the group relationships, review the accomplishments of the year, or give special attention to ways in which the members have assumed responsibilities and different types of leadership. The committee may study the group in one or all of these ways and make its report.

Questions to guide the evaluation are found in Chapters One and Three. In Chapter One, a "Measuring Stick" was given for our visit through the church school. The same measuring stick could be adapted for study of one's own group, eliminating only question 1 and changing the words "pupils" to "members," and "teacher" to "leader" where the group is not a class. That we can use the same measuring stick for a class, a hobby group, and an adult society or club is another indication of the wider horizons in educational thinking. It demonstrates again the philosophy that teaching is a fellowship between teacher and pupils and a process whereby the teacher helps the pupils to grow as competent, dedicated, creative persons living in the community. It is a recognition of the fact that all Christian groups will have this same ultimate goal.

The marks of a functioning group, developed in Chapter Three, can be used as a guide in evaluation. The committee, or the group, can ask itself about each of these marks:

1. To what degree do we have a uniting of minds?
2. What evidence have we that our members desire to grow?
3. To what degree do our members share in planning our activities?
4. Is decision making a difficult process, or have we learned when we can reach decision quickly and when we must wait?
5. Do our members have a genuine interest in each other?
6. Are we regular in attendance and meeting?
7. What significant accomplishments of the group can we name?
8. Have we found our interest going on from one study or activity into the next?

From the Study of Groups to a Study of Techniques

Developing an understanding of individuals and their relationships is essential for the group leader. His concern is first of all for persons. He seeks also to develop in persons a concern for one another and for the success of the group. As the leader, however, he must also develop the skills of guiding discussion and stimulating thought.

CHAPTER V

THE ART OF DISCUSSION

DISCUSSION IS THE BASIC ART IN GROUP LEADERSHIP. WE have all had some experience with discussion, yet we need to ask ourselves the difference between discussion and debate, argument, questions and answers, or free conversation. In a debate or argument I try to prove that I am right and that you are wrong. We take sides on an issue on which we differ. In the question-and-answer technique the leader asks questions to which he has the answers. In free conversation we talk about anything which comes to mind and move freely to other topics without purpose or goal.

Discussion is none of these. It is a meeting of minds searching for insight or understanding on a problem, a felt need, or a matter of common interest. There is no discussion of a specific fact. Does the book have a red cover? Who was the first president of our country? Where did the Wright brothers make their famous flight? Discussion centers around how and why and the implications. It is concerned with what we think and with what plans we need to make.

In thinking together, each gives and each receives. We are concerned with a problem. We want to give our own ideas about it, but we also want to hear what others think. When someone else shares a thought, our own thoughts grow. Our minds are active as we work over the problem together. At the end of the discussion we may all agree on a solution that was better than any one of us could have conceived. We may not find a common solution, but each of us has some new material with which to think. Each has grown in the process.

The discussion begins with a clear statement of the problem to be considered. Let us take a group approaching the practical problem of what specific service activity to take up for Christmas. Several individuals, or a committee, have been investigating possibilities and needs. They report their findings. The group has already decided to do something. The matter for discussion is, what shall we do? The members of the group asks questions, share ideas, consider their own limitations and their interests. Finally they agree on a specific project. Their next step is to make definite plans for action.

Now someone will say, "Why didn't the committee recommend one plan and let the group vote on it? They probably would accept the recommendation and they could have saved a lot of time!" Such an objector has either had an unpleasant experience with poor group discussion—of which there are unfortunately too many—or he is not aware of the values to be gained in group concentration on the problem. Everybody who shared in the discussion of what to do has begun to take an active interest in the problem. Already the project has become our project, not the committee's. When it comes to planning for action, we are all ready to help. The thinking, the reasoning, and the decision were ours. We are ready to undertake the work.

There are techniques to be understood if a discussion is to be pleasant and profitable. It is imperative that the leader understand these techniques, and equally important that he help his group to learn them. He must understand first of all that whether the group is his Sunday-school class, his young-people's meeting, or a group of his own peers, he is not "teaching" them in discussion. He is among them as an instrument whose function is to make each person's best thinking available to the group. In discussion his own ideas about the problem are the least important of all. He is like the outstanding football player who becomes a referee. From that moment his job is to keep the game moving according to the rules, to see that each player shall have a fair chance, and that fouls be caught at once. The only time he takes the ball is when he sets it back in play. His mind is on the ball and the players. He is there every second. But he keeps out of the way as much as possible.

A diagram of group discussion shows that it goes

This Way: **Not This Way:**

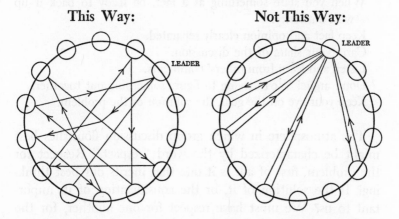

In the discussion the leader's job is to focus attention on the problem, throw it out to the group, and let them toss it back and forth. He re-enters the discussion if someone goes off on a tangent. The leader comes to the rescue of the person whose contribution is in danger of being lost. He tries to draw out those who are slow to speak. Occasionally, where necessary, he gives a quick résumé of what has been said. When the time is up or enough has been said, he tries to lift up what seems to be agreed on for the consensus of the group. It is important for the group to know that this is the function of the leader.

A group of young people who realized that their group discussion needed polishing came up with these guides:

Understand the problem.
Stick to the problem.
Be specific when you speak.
If you have a good illustration, give it briefly.
If you have some facts we need, out with them.
When you state something as a fact, be ready to back it up
  with authority.
Keep fact and opinion clearly separated.
Carry your share of the discussion.
Listen and learn from others' comments.
Don't argue! We're trying to figure something out together.
Keep your eye on the goal, the solution of the problem.

The atmosphere in which group discussion flourishes best might be characterized by the word "respect." Respect for the problem, first of all. Is it one that merits our best thinking? Is the solution of it, or the consideration of it, important to us? We must have respect for one another, for the thinking, the ideas, and the consideration of ideas which each has to give. Certainly we must have respect for the leader and he for us. And we must have respect for each contribution made, the least, the most faltering, and the most fluent. Finally we must have respect for ourselves.

Otherwise we say, "Oh, I have nothing to contribute. I'll just listen to the others."

Planning for group discussion is more difficult than planning to make a speech. The good leader prepares for anything that may arise. He thinks and reads in the area of the discussion. He tries to imagine the solutions at which the group may arrive. He thinks of all the questions and issues that should be included. He plans questions for stimulating or furthering the discussion—questions which he may never have to use. Adequate preparation makes him feel at ease with the problem and enables him to concentrate on the members of the group.

Look at two questions that point up the difference between good and poor questions: Is the book cover red? Why is the book cover red? The one requires simply a yes-or-no answer. The other digs into meanings and reasons. Questions that ask: "What do you think? Why do you think so? How do you think this might be done?" are all questions which lead the speaker on to express his thoughts. Questions should be unbiased; that is, they should not indicate what the leader thinks or expects in answer. The best questions are addressed to the topic or to the group in general, not to one specific person. When discussion is lively, the group members will question each other.

The leader sees to it that adequate material is on hand in case there may be need to refer to it. He may ask a committee or an individual to bring this in, but he sees that it is there. The committee presenting facts about Christmas projects might bring in literature from agencies or institutions in which there is interest. The teacher who wants to discuss with her juniors, "How shall we make the study of Joseph interesting?" will have pictures of dioramas, of Egypt, of

83

archaeological discoveries, books about Joseph, perhaps one on making a play, one on making models, literature from a museum, a Bible commentary, and any other models or books which she thinks may be useful. She does not set out to have the children make a series of dioramas. Her material suggests that thought, but it also suggests many other thoughts. She has set the stage for their thinking.

The leader also thinks about the individuals in his group. How will this problem appeal to them? Will they take it up as important? Is there someone who is likely to throw cold water on every idea? What might be used to appeal to him? Is there someone who already takes such a definite stand on the problem that he will need to be toned down or kept in check while others present different ideas? The leader thinks of each person's relation to the problem and his probable responses.

Finally, the leader plans exactly how he will begin the discussion. That much is easy! Concluding the discussion satisfactorily and with what the comedian calls a "punch line" is much more difficult. Not knowing what solution the group will reach is only part of the problem. The leader wonders whether the discussion will move with humor and friendliness, or whether someone in the group will give an unfriendly tone to the proceedings. Finishing a discussion properly leaves the group with a feeling of satisfaction at what has been accomplished, or it may leave them with a challenge to get at the problem again in their next session, or it may raise their determination to act and send them off with a high sense of dedication.

For example, the leader of the Christmas-project discussion might have for his use a poem, a prayer, a hymn, or even a story. He may use none of these. As the discussion draws to a close, by sensing the feeling of the group, he will decide which one of them or what else will give the right touch. Or take the teacher of juniors. She may have a passage from the Bible in mind to read at the close. Perhaps she has a picture of Joseph for the children to look at quietly for a moment. She may be thinking of some words that she will shape into a prayer according to the need. When we finish a good book, we lay it down with a sigh. What a disappointment if the ending is not as exciting or well written as the beginning or the middle!

The leader, then, may think of the discussion as having three parts: the opening, the body, and the conclusion. She plans an opening that will catch interest immediately. She plans materials and questions that will be used as needed to guide the group through the discussion. And she plans a conclusion that is flexible but that will give a finish, a polish, to the time spent thinking together.

The teacher or leader who wants to build a functioning group will practice the techniques of discussion. As she grows in the art—and it is an art—she will begin to feel the joy of watching thoughts develop and find expression. There will be satisfaction in drawing out the quiet one and in helping the aggressive member to take his rightful place as one of the group. The sense of fellowship that will spring up between leader and group will add richness to the lives of all.

There are certain guides or cautions which may help in the early stages of group discussion. The first of these is that the leader must be sure the group sets boundaries. In a young group this is closely related to behavior. The young people who listed the guides for "polishing" their group discussions had learned by experience some of the boundaries that needed to be set. To these we might add:

85

If there is a time limitation, have a clock in full view.

Agree that only one person speaks at a time.

Agree that whatever is said is said to the whole group.

When two people try to speak at once, let the one who last spoke wait.

Members talk to the group, not to the leader.

The important thing is that the boundaries be set by the group. Some leader will ask, "What if they don't list all these boundaries?" Of course they won't the first time! As they gain experience they will see other rules to add to the list. The leader's job is to help the group face its difficulties, evaluate, and restate the rules as needed.

Another caution concerns the quiet person. Some groups are never satisfied until every person speaks in the discussion. Other groups feel that there are times when someone may participate with much silent thinking yet not speak. The first group answers, "How can you tell? If the person is thinking and he is part of the group, he has a responsibility to share his thinking to help the rest of us." They might also say, "How can we help him if we do not know what he is thinking?" And the teacher whose aim is to help each child grow must reach out toward the quiet child until that child feels secure enough, wanted enough, respected enough, to make his contribution. Let the teacher put herself in the place of that child, look at teacher and group through that child's eyes, and she will begin to understand the child and reach him.

Adult groups content with a lecture are missing the interchange of thought which comes through discussion. It is not laziness which sets the stage for lecturing. It is misinterpretation of how learning takes place and a lack of skill at facilitating participation. The adult Bible class can be as stimulat-

86

ing and active a learning group as any other in the church if its leaders will study group discussion and employ some of the techniques for fuller participation in large groups. A youth group has been used in this chapter to illustrate the development of a group's ability to discuss. An adult group or a children's group can approach the need for better discussion in the same way. Skill in group discussion would mean better woman's society meetings, better board meetings, better committee meetings, and would lead to more effective group action generally.

When the group plans for action, the most important caution is this: Whose idea is it? Many a teacher has felt quite pleased with herself when her group took up an idea of hers which she thought was good. All too soon in some cases the teacher was "holding the bag." As one youngster expressed it, "It's her idea. Let her do it!" The teacher has ideas, yes. When her group is new, she will have to suggest ideas. At least let her start with several ideas so that the choice may belong to the group. We feed the child for a while, but soon he takes up the spoon himself.

And so the next caution has to do with a guiding or a restraining hand. It is difficult to speak of this caution when one has seen a group do things which the leader thought were too difficult. Some young people carried on a neighborhood project all one summer with adult leadership that was not too strong. Day after day the young people were on hand with games and crafts ready. The direction was largely in the hands of a keen-minded, dedicated high-school boy with whom the leader was sensible enough to go along.

A group of intermediates went to the police and got permission to hold a parade. Permission was granted, they organized the parade, and carried it through successfully. The leader afterward confessed that she was scared of the bigness of the project when it was suggested and amazed at the "nerve" of the boys and girls in going to the police. "They insisted they could, and they did!"

A group in which there were just six active intermediates got out a church newspaper every week for a year, doing most of the typographical work and all the writing themselves. Sometimes there was only a single page, sometimes four, but every week the paper was distributed. And their leader thought the job was too much, that they would quit, or at least go on a monthly basis before long.

On the other hand, these groups are experienced. The leader starting with a new group will have to be fairly sure that what they plan can be accomplished. Accomplishment is necessary to the group. Failure can be disintegrating. Planning must be based on purposeful thinking and good discussion.

The problem very often is one of stimulating thought. Most groups do not leap into a discussion without some preparation and guidance. Yet too often a leader will say, "My group just won't discuss. They sit here and say nothing." There are ways of creating an atmosphere and building a readiness for discussion. Some of the techniques are presented in the next chapter.

CHAPTER VI

STIMULATING THOUGHT

THE TITLE OF THIS CHAPTER IS NOT MEANT TO IMPLY THAT you will find here a stimulating thought, though it is to be hoped that you may. Rather, the title implies that one of our basic jobs as leaders of groups is to stimulate the thinking of those about us. Teachers of classes, those who have responsibility in the women's groups, chairmen of committees and boards, and all others with positions of leadership, get co-operation and perform their jobs well when they know how to start and guide the thinking process. Thinking together produces greater interest and shared responsibility for the learning and doing.

By what practical means do we stimulate the thinking of others? Consider for a moment the ministry of Jesus. Constantly he sought to reach men's minds. He asked them, "What do you think?" "How do you read the law?" "What say you?" He took the wheat in his hands for them to see. He pointed to a woman depositing a coin in the temple. He told a story and then asked the listener to point up the meaning. His illustrations came from the common things of life, the things people knew but seldom considered. He met people where they were in their thinking and challenged them to move forward.

Think of your group and the job you have to do. You may

be in charge of the program at a meeting, chairman of a committee to study some problem, the superintendent preparing for a meeting of workers, or the teacher of a Sunday-morning class. Is your group already thinking about the problem or the material at hand? Do you know what they think about it, or must you start their thinking? Where are they mentally and spiritually?

When you invite a missionary who has returned from a foreign land to speak to your group, he usually brings with him some articles from that land to display. Your people finger the objects and ask questions about them. They are starting to think about the faraway land. Perhaps the missionary brings slides or movies of the station where he worked. If he uses these successfully, he causes you to think about the people and their problems. His aim is not to entertain, but to make you desire to be a part of the Church's outreach. How well he succeeds with you, only you can tell. Unless he stirs the minds of his listeners, he will not succeed at all.

Have you ever attended a teachers' meeting to which an "expert" has been invited? Perhaps he has been widely heralded as one who knows all the problems and has the answers. Poor fellow! Two strikes against him before he starts! Most of us resent experts who come in to tell us how we should do things. The person who really helps us is the one who looks at our problems with us and then guides us to finding our own solutions. If he can lead us to the place where we say what can be done and what ought to be done, he will have done us a great service. We will have put ourselves on record and we are, therefore, likely to do something about the problems. Perhaps we should immediately sign up this outside leader to come back a year later and check up.

There was once a cartoon, now happily lost in the dim past, which showed a child with the top of his head lifted up like the lid of a jar. Beside the child stood a benevolent adult filling the open-topped head from a pitcher marked "Knowledge." Some people still think that education is like that. The teacher comes into the class on Sunday morning and delivers a lecture. Whether the supposedly open-topped head is eight or eighty, it won't work! Telling is not teaching, and listening is seldom learning.

Thinking is the essential element in learning. How can we start the thinking process? How can we guide it? How can we bring about the interchange of thoughts within the group, so that we may "reason together" and grow?

Put It on Paper

Miss Evans and her class had studied a unit of work on Christian vocation. Toward the end of the unit the material suggested a discussion of the question, "What is success?" "A good topic," thought Miss Evans, "especially in such a unit as this. How shall I be sure that we get everyone's thinking about it? How can I be sure to have all thoughts shared and none lost?"

The plan she developed was simple. When the class assembled, she had pencils and paper ready for all. "Let's try an experiment in words this morning," she said. "We've been studying vocations and thinking about our work in the world. You have some ideas about the kinds of jobs you want. I'm sure every one of you wants to be a success. That's the word I'd like us to experiment with this morning—success. What does it mean? What's your definition? Without letting anyone see what you write, will you each complete this sentence, using as many or as few words as you want." She turned to a large sheet of paper on the wall and wrote in black crayon: "Success means . . ."

For several minutes pencils were busy, either as an aid to thought by being chewed on, or in setting down thoughts on paper. When everyone had written something and most were finished, Miss Evans led the group in sharing their thoughts and discussing the idea. Each person had something to offer. Each one had thought.

This device is so simple that it can be used with any age or size of group so long as the participants can write. In a large group there will not be opportunity to hear from everyone, but the pencil, the paper, and the straightforward direction will start the thinking process. When the leader and others speak, there will be a readiness to hear and to check others' thoughts with those we have set on paper ourselves. In any group the person who hesitates to speak will be freer to do so when he has his thoughts set before him in black and white.

Guided Silent Reading

Two classes sat near each other in the crowded church auditorium. Heads were bent over books in both classes. From one class came the drone of voice after voice taking turns reading the lesson. From the other class not a sound was heard for several minutes. Then the teacher asked quietly, "Well, what did you find out?" Response was immediate and eager. In their own words and with some enthusiasm in their voices this class discussed the question the answer to which they had been seeking in their reading.

Ask the first class, "Why are you reading the lesson?" They will probably tell you, "We're supposed to." Ask the same question of the second class and they will tell you, "To find out something." Are we reading words or thinking thoughts?

The teacher of the class which had read silently had given them two questions and told them they would find the answers in certain paragraphs in their books. Reading to find something, they were reading thoughtfully.

In introducing a study of Paul's letter to the Galatians, a teacher of an adult Bible class asked the class to read to themselves the first nine verses of the letter and find out why Paul was writing. As each person discovered the problem which the churches of Galatia were facing, questions arose. The class wanted to find out who the false preachers were who were unsettling Paul's followers. They were ready to find out what the false doctrines were and how Paul dealt with them. The letter, the ancient Church, and the study had come alive. Through guided silent reading thinking had begun.

Most lesson materials give the teacher suggestions for guiding the class in this way. Questions are given in the teacher's material and sometimes in the pupil's book as well. In most cases the purpose of the questions is not merely to gather fact, but rather to stimulate thoughtful reading. The use we make of the thinking which is thus begun will depend on the skill we have developed in guiding discussion.

The Browsing Table

The browsing table, too, is supposed to stimulate thinking. How often it does will depend on how carefully the materials on it have been selected and how well they are used. Some teachers prefer the name research table, study table, or resource table. These names are more descriptive of the proper use of such materials. The browsing table should contain resource materials related to the study or which relate the study to the lives of the class. Materials should be contributed by class members as well as by the teacher. The one who brings any such contribution should tell about it. A rich and inviting table will include pictures, newspaper clippings, magazine articles, marked paragraphs in books, objects, maps, and bits of information typed on filing cards. The resource table will grow as the study grows.

"Sounds good," said a teacher one night at a meeting, "but I scarcely have room to get my class in. I haven't the space for another table."

"Would you really like to make use of resource materials in this way?" asked the leader.

"Well, yes," came the answer a little hesitantly, "but . . ."

"Let's think about it," said the leader turning to the group at the meeting. "How could such material be collected and used without benefit of table?"

There was a moment of silence. Then came several good suggestions. The group agreed that in such circumstances it would probably be necessary to limit the material to pictures, clippings, small pamphlets, and information typed on cards or paper. Such material, they said, could be carried in a brief case and passed around. Or it could be organized in folders in a cardboard file box. Mount the clippings and pictures on the pages of a large loose-leaf notebook, said another, and also keep the information on such pages. Then the material wouldn't be falling on the floor, and it would be easy to turn from page to page for the piece you wanted.

"You can do almost anything if you want to badly enough," observed a teacher of many years. The group smiled and nodded agreement.

There is, of course, no sense having a browsing or resource table unless it is used. The teacher will be making good use of time and materials if she meets early comers at the table. Studying pictures for details, finding information to be shared later, discussing new materials, all help the class members to recall last week's session and to start thinking toward this one. Opportunity should be made to refer to the materials on the table during the class session. When this is the practice of the class, members will go to the material to illustrate a point or to bring in new information.

The browsing table has its place in other meetings besides class sessions. The active superintendent places the table in a prominent place at the workers' conference. Sometimes he puts one teacher in charge of it, and she is responsible for drawing other workers into conversation about the materials. Just as the teacher asks a pupil to find something on the table to share, so the superintendent will guide early comers toward the material and point out a pamphlet or clipping that may have bearing on discussion in the meeting.

In business meetings of the governing board of the church or the woman's organization the browsing table is an excellent means of drawing indirect attention to the work or the problems of the church school, the community, or the church at large. Make the table attractive, keep it timely, keep it centered around one idea or theme. Have someone posted to direct attention to it and someone prepared to enter into discussion of the materials on it. The browsing table, wisely used, is an excellent means of stimulating thought.

Groups Within Groups

During the past few years the term "buzz groups" has come into frequent use. The technique is used, particularly in large groups, as a means of giving everyone an opportunity to talk. The large group is broken up into small groups of six or eight persons. This grouping is done quickly and informally by asking everyone to get with such a group in his immediate vicinity, no group to exceed a certain number. A question is raised or a controversial statement is made in the large group. The leader then asks everyone to discuss the matter in the small groups. When the total group is reassembled, each small unit shares through one or more spokesmen the thoughts expressed in the buzz session.

The advantages of such a procedure are many. The small face-to-face group gives everyone a chance to express himself. The timid person, who may have an important contribution, but who would never speak up in a large assembly, shares his thoughts with a group of six or eight. Encouraged by their reception, he may share with the total group. If not, someone in his unit may tell of his contribution. As the six or eight talk together, each one pushes himself to voice his thoughts. In other words, he thinks. The possible monotony of sitting and listening for a half-hour or more is broken. Instead of being receivers and spectators, the members become participants.

On the other hand we need to face the fact that such a procedure does not just happen. If buzz groups are a new experience to most of our members, we need to give explicit, though brief, directions. "This is the way we get into groups; we simply turn our chairs. Or we huddle over the back of a pew. We do not get up and move." Perhaps we need to state the discussion procedure: "Stick to the topic. Only one person speak at a time. Give everyone a chance. Don't argue. Try to understand everyone's viewpoint. Don't get sidetracked. Keep your voices low."

We need to be specific about what is to be discussed and set limits on it. For example, the question, "What is the function of the Church?" is far too broad to be handled in buzz groups. But the question, "What can we as Christian church people do about a certain immediate community problem?" should be discussed in small groups where everyone can speak. The "certain problem," of course, would be presented first to the total body. Suggestions and action proposals growing out of the buzz sessions might become the basis for a second set of small group discussions. If the problem is one on which the whole group wants to act, some consensus as to a starting point and a plan will begin to emerge. Since everyone has had an opportunity to express himself in the meeting, there will be greater unanimity and conviction when the meeting is over.

In the church-school class there are many ways of working in subgroups. An intermediate class was working on a unit about ideas of God in the Old Testament. The immediate topic was symbols used in the psalms to express the people's ideas about God. The class of twelve was divided into four subgroups of three persons each. Each subgroup was given several psalms to examine for symbols. Each was to check its list to eliminate any duplications and to be ready to explain the meaning attached to each symbol. In the twenty-five minutes so used, everyone was busy and thinking. Each one felt a responsibility to his small group. Many more psalms were covered than would have been possible with one group of twelve. Everyone shared in discussing the meanings of the symbols. In other words, in small groups properly set in motion, we get more thinking by more people and better results.

Suppose a youth group decides to study "social welfare in our city." The members compile a list of a dozen or more agencies at work in this field. Is it reasonable to expect the entire group to visit all agencies? Will they accomplish their purposes better if a number of small groups each visits one or more agencies? Are there advantages to having a group of four rather than one individual make a visit?

When study groups contain more than eight persons, we need to ask ourselves such questions. Our purpose, be it recalled, is to help people grow. The larger the group, the more likely we are to lose sight of the individual. And the harder it is for the individual to make himself heard and his needs felt; the easier it becomes for him to sit back as a nonparticipant.

Surveys and Interviews

We can draw the members of our groups into active, thoughtful participation through the use of surveys and interviews. Not every problem or unit of work lends itself to this technique, but this is a means of getting variety into our methods and of relating ourselves and our work to those about us. This is action study, and a high degree of interest surrounds it.

How often have we undertaken a study of "our church" with any age group, and confined ourselves to the book and the classroom?

A slight commotion was heard in the hall of a large church one Sunday morning. The superintendent stepped to the doorway of the office and watched. Two by two on tiptoe the nursery children were climbing the stairs to the small room where the sexton would pull the bell rope to send the chimes pealing out over the town. At the head of the stairs stood the man whom they had met before as a helper. He was tall and smiling and had a word of greeting for each one. They told him they had heard the bell on other Sundays and they wanted to see him ring it. The sexton held a little boy up and let him try to pull the rope.

"Unh! It's hard," grunted the little fellow, all eyes upon him.

The sexton set the boy down and got out his watch. He told the children he must pull the bell rope at just the right time to call the people to church. Then putting the watch in his pocket, he grasped the rope in his lean, strong fingers. Pull and release. Pull and release. The children bent their bodies in a rhythm matching his. Hands reached up, and soon all were playing the game of ringing the bell as they had done many times in their room. The teacher sang their church-bell song in rhythm with the sexton's pull. When the last note died away, several of the children took the sexton's hands, and he walked with them to their room.

Was it an interview? Did the children learn about their church and one of its workers? Did they grow in their love for the church through this happy experience? Which of them would ever hear the church bells again without seeing the tall, kindly man who pulled the rope, or without having a sense of belonging? "That's my church. I saw the man pull the rope."

The primary class we visited in Chapter One was preparing for an interview with their minister. Older boys and girls seek out church officials and inquire about their part in the work of the church. We visit other churches, survey those in our communities and our jobs. Actually we stimulate not only our own thinking, but theirs also.

The procedure? First, we state our purposes again clearly. What are we trying to find out? Is our search important enough to take the time of busy people? With primaries and juniors we then list some of the questions we want to ask. With older groups we may make up a questionnaire.

An intermediate group went out in pairs in their various communities one Sunday afternoon to ask some church members they knew about their Bibles and what use was made of them at home. They had such questions as these: Do you have a family Bible? Do you have an old Bible with an interesting history or a Bible in another language? What are some of your favorite passages? When do you read the Bible? How do you use it at home?

The questions accomplished many things. The intermediates thought about their own Bibles and how they used them at home. The people who were questioned did some thinking. What some of them shared helped the boys and girls to see the importance of this book to older people whom they knew. In a few homes the intermediates found little use of the Bible. When they had compiled the results, they discussed their findings with the minister. He appreciated the worthwhileness of what they were doing and made use of some of their information in subsequent sermons.

A young-adult group raised questions about Christian relationships in business. They interviewed employers and employees in the offices, factories, and stores where they worked. They used their findings to draw some conclusions and to state some principles about working together. A copy of the results was sent to everyone interviewed. No one could measure the results of such a study, but the group had a feeling that they had made a contribution to the community.

Quizzes and Tests

In earlier days the primary motivation for learning in the classroom was the test. Rewards, whether in the form of marks, something more tangible, or the glory of winning, followed. Education today depends on a higher type of motivation. We recognize that boys and girls, as well as men and women, do want to learn and achieve. Education is built around learning for use and for living. We start a unit by asking ourselves, "Why is this learning important to us?" What then of tests?

We use tests today in order to find out our weaknesses. We use them to evaluate progress in terms of goals that we have set.

A senior-high group set out to study the New Testament. They agreed that it was important and that they did not know enough about it. In discussion they shared what they knew. Then the teacher said, "I have here a test that covers many of the facts about the New Testament and the major teachings in it. Would you like to test yourselves and then set goals for what we want to learn about this portion of our Bible?"

The group liked the idea. Here was a test with a purpose. There was nothing to be afraid of in taking this test. There would be no passing or failing, but through the test they could determine the limits of their knowledge and information which they needed. So the test was taken. The boys and girls checked their papers together and listed the areas in which they needed to study. At the end of the study someone suggested that they take the test again. This time it was used to evaluate their progress.

At the end of a unit a junior-class teacher said, "Let's make up some quiz questions to see how much we have learned." She suggested that the class divide into two groups, and that each group should check back through the unit and list ten questions. Each group would then try to answer the questions of the other group. The class liked the plan. They discussed the kinds of information and the ideas which should be covered by the questions. They agreed that "trick" questions would not help them to see what had been learned. They recalled their objectives in the study and decided to plan questions that would call for important learnings. The teacher divided her time between the two groups, helping them to phrase ideas when they got stuck and leading them on to look at all areas of the study. When they came back the following Sunday to quiz each other, interest was high. The questions were good and so were the answers. When it was over, the general feeling was expressed by a boy who said, "Gee, we learned a lot, didn't we?"

In both these classes the boys and girls were saying in effect, "We are trying to learn something." This is quite different from the teacher giving the test to judge the work of the individuals. The boys and girls used the tests thoughtfully. The checkup was both a stimulus and an aid to thinking.

Interpreting Hymns and Pictures

On an easel before the group was a large picture portraying Jesus and a young man. The leader sat down with the group. Along with the group he looked at the picture. For a moment no one spoke. Then the leader said, "What do you think Jesus may be saying to the young man?" Again there was silence, and the leader waited. He was not afraid to give them time to think. Finally someone broke the silence and a good discussion followed.

Suppose the leader had begun with an interpretation of what he thought the Master was saying. The group would probably have listened and thought along with him. But would they have been using their own minds creatively? Some of them might, but the technique of throwing the burden of thought on the group first is a surer way of stimulating original thought.

What about the leader's preparation for such a use of a picture? Does he simply set the picture up and wait for what may come from the group? Not if he is a good teacher! In his time of preparation he himself thinks about the picture. He reads the interpretation of it in one or more of the many books of picture interpretations. He looks at it through the eyes of each member of his group. He thinks, "What will Joe see in this picture? What will Sue's reaction be?" He gets himself ready and receptive to hear the group's ideas and to lead them on.

In the same way a familiar or a new hymn can be used. The words of a hymn often have different meanings to different persons. Take such a hymn as "Fight the Good Fight," and discuss the question, "What do the words 'the good fight' mean to you?" Each person in the group will have his own interpretation, but will his thought not be enriched by hearing the ideas of others?

Or take the introduction of a hymn that is new to the group and draw out the word pictures that each can see. When the juniors learn the hymn, "Book of Books, Our People's Strength," it is one thing for the leader to tell them about the prophets and statesmen. It is a far more significant experience for the juniors, with the teacher's guidance, to draw upon their own background, and find for themselves some of the understandings which give reality to the words. Further, by this process we are teaching worshipers to sing all hymns more thoughtfully.

Mind Activators and the Group

We have spoken of a number of techniques which might be called "mind activators," those means by which we stimulate thinking. We have tried also to show that thinking together produces richer results than thinking alone. This may not be true of the genius and is probably not true in technical areas where an individual has attained expert status. Even here, if the expert can discuss with other experts, his thinking will surely be challenged beyond what he could do alone.

In matters with which we deal in the church school—Christian living and growing—it can be stated quite positively on the basis of experiences common to all that when we share our thinking and work at a problem together, the results are more far reaching than when we think alone. The very act of putting our thoughts into words makes us more conscious of them and more specific about them. The reactions of others to our thoughts—with either challenge or confirmation—refine and deepen our thinking. Coming to certain affirmations in fellowship with others gives not only satisfaction, but also strength. We go forth in the conviction that we stand not alone but are part of the company of the faith.

Thinking is the basic activity. Without thinking little learning can take place. The leader who works with groups and believes that learning is something which the learner must do will use every means possible to stimulate thinking and to promote thoughtful participation in discussion.

CHAPTER VII

GROUPS AT PLAY

RECREATION, DRAMATICS, AND CHORAL SPEAKING ARE
three types of activities which provide full opportunity for
creative thinking, group planning, and fellowship building.
They are presented in the next three chapters as specific examples of the ways in which groups can function effectively in
a wide variety of church-school situations.

Much has been said about the importance of play in the
life of the family. We have all heard the couplet:

> The family that plays together
> Stays together.

The thought may well be applied to the program of the
church. Busy as we are with lessons and programs and business
and worship, recreation too often trails behind as a pleasant
but unnecessary activity. Youth groups, to their credit, insist
on having fun, and most of our recreational endeavors are
directed toward them. Occasional parties for the children, tea
and cookies for the adults, round out the recreational programs
of too many churches.

The word is inclusive. Anything which relaxes the mind
or body, creates fun and laughter, gives pleasure and fellowship is recreation. As spectators we enjoy television, movies,

105

concerts, sports, and all manner of programs put on for our entertainment. There is the need, however, to play the game ourselves, to participate. No pictures of mountain climbing or deep-sea-diving movie can give the exhilaration of an afternoon hike and the pleasure of the hot dog we ourselves have cooked over an open fire.

Play breaks down barriers. When we play with people, we learn what they are. Hidden corners of their personality are opened to us, just as we are opened to them. Shared laughter creates a bond between us. To the church-school leader this is a point to be marked. We want to help the individuals in our group to grow. To do this we must know them and establish a friendly relationship with them. Play is not the only way, but it is a very good way to accomplish this goal.

Having fun together is one of the best ways of building unity and solidarity in our group. The wise teacher plans an outing or party with her group at the very beginning of the church-school year. Though it may cost her an afternoon or an evening, the results will prove its worth. The church-school superintendent who plans carefully for sociability at his autumn workers' conference will be developing teamwork among his staff. Especially important is this in a large church where the workers may not know each other well. Greetings on Sunday morning will be friendlier, interest in each other will be greater, and attendance at subsequent conferences will be better.

There are two major obstacles working against recreational activities within the church. One is the pressure of conflicting interests, and the other is distance. These obstacles are equally true of both rural and urban churches. It is the unusual church whose families live within walking distance. It is even more unusual to find a church whose families are not pulled this way and that by school, community affairs, social engagements, clubs, campaigns, and the like. Even the youngest school children have their dancing classes, music lessons, cub packs, brownie troops, art lessons, and clubs. And how the activities multiply with the years!

Shall the church add to the confusion by setting up still more activities? Shall we be content with two or three hours on Sunday plus the work of the woman's society? However plain the answers may seem, these questions are not easy to answer. Whoever calls a meeting or a social gathering without due regard to purpose is trifling with all-important time. Not until we get back to a clear-cut statement of our objectives can we be sure of the direction our recreational activities should take.

Have we forgotten the primary function of the church? We are trying to lead persons into the kingdom of God. That is, we are trying to develop persons who will love God with heart and mind and soul and strength, and their neighbors as themselves. Are we accomplishing that goal under our present program? If we are, then nothing further is needed, and we will not add to the confusion of our times with more activities.

When we examine recreation in the light of our objectives, we gain a new sense of direction. Our planning becomes more purposeful. We ask: "How can this party or dinner or program help our people to grow? What activities do we need to include to help us to achieve our goals?"

Similarly, we look at the results. What did this party accomplish? Did these boys grow as Christians because of their participation in our sports program? What did this dinner contribute toward the building of better persons and a better world? These matters are rightly the concern of every leader and of the commission on education in the local church.

The recreation program can be as rich and varied as we wish to make it. Activities are organized around the age groups, around special interests, and around the family unit. Let us examine some of these with a desire to improve our working techniques and to explore new avenues of fruitful endeavor.

What About Parties?

A teacher of intermediates planned a party for her boys and girls. She announced the date. She spent time in preparation, planned some games, and fixed refreshments. Nobody came. The teacher, in a mixture of irritation and despair, was ready to give up her class. A wise superintendent helped her to see what had happened.

It was not that the boys and girls disliked their teacher or parties. The error lay in the planning. The party was all the teacher's doing. In all sincerity of purpose, but with a lack of understanding of intermediates, the teacher had planned, invited, and prepared. She had not taken account of the other activities of her class. More important, she had overlooked the fact that young people do not want things done for them. They welcome activities with adults, but to have a party planned for them is "kid stuff."

At the other extreme, a teacher who let her intermediates do all the planning had a full attendance but a highly disorganized party. The boys and girls brought enough food and soft drinks for three parties. Lack of co-operation spoiled the games. There were a few awkward attempts at dancing. Finally the party deteriorated into a rough house and the teacher said, "Never again!"

Both of these teachers had felt the importance of parties. They gave their time willingly in order that they and their classes might have fun together. They hoped to increase the friendliness and the good relationships within the class and between themselves and their classes. They hoped that the parties might help their boys and girls have fun under the auspices of the church and grow in their understanding of Christian recreation. Judged by outcomes, both parties were failures.

Good party planning follows the same principles as all other successful work with groups. Let us watch the procedure of a teacher who thinks that a party would help his class to become more united, to grow in friendliness, and who sees a need to help them learn how to plan times of fun.

"What do you people do for fun?" he asks them.

The replies indicate movies, television, the roller-skating rink, getting together at the drugstore, going to football games and occasionally to dances, as the chief social pursuits of these junior-highs.

"What about parties?" asks the teacher.

"Oh, parties!" The answer is almost a groan. "You sit around and play games and then somebody wants to play post office. The best thing about parties is the food."

"We had a party at junior-high camp that was fun, though," says one boy. "We had stunts and charades and some contests. We never stopped the whole evening and everybody had a swell time."

"Yeah," says a boy who went with him. "That was fun. If we could do something like that now, . . ."

"Well, why can't we?" says the teacher. "You don't have a party like that without planning, but it's worth it."

Some of the boys and girls are enthusiastic, some dubious, but all are willing to go along. Suggestions are made for games and stunts that could be fun. They talk about food, the time,

109

and the place for the party. They want to hold it at the church and they set a date. Responsibilities are delegated. A committee of three is to get the food agreed on by the group and take charge of serving and cleaning up. Everybody will share the cost and a limit is set. Two of the members will take care of the room arrangement and the "atmosphere." This consists of setting up a serving table with a cloth, candles, and bouquet, and bringing a record player to provide music at the beginning of the party and during refreshments. Several others are given responsibility for taking charge of the activities. One of the girls is selected as general chairman. She will check up on the others and see that all jobs are taken care of. The teacher will work with her and help out where needed. The teacher's role in the planning has been that of guide or counselor. He has helped the group to evaluate suggestions that are made. He has helped them to reach decisions through discussion and then to plan responsibilities. He has been an interested participant in the group in such a way that the plans are not his but the group's.

The party that grew out of this planning was a complete success. The records set the tone for a gay evening. In the first activity each person, including the teacher, had the name of a comic-strip character pinned on his back. By asking questions of the others, he had to find out who he was. Although it was not in the planning, each one assumed the role of that character for the rest of the evening. The second activity was a "hockey" game, played with a ping-pong ball on a small table. The group was divided into two teams standing on opposite sides of the table. The object was to blow the ball off the opposing team's side. No hands, of course. Just blowing. Red faces and helpless laughter attested the success of this. "Steal the Bacon" followed, providing a few calmer

110

moments. Then came a form of charades. After that chairs were placed in a circle, and there was a series of games like "Coffeepot," or "Boots Without Shoes," in which "it" had to guess the trick in order to be successful. Finally, while the refreshment committee got to work, each of the others was given a bag of materials, including two pipe cleaners, a rag, a marshmallow, a clothespin, six cloves, two toothpicks, a feather, a piece of string, and some colored crepe paper. The instructions were to use any or all of this and make a statue, a figure, or an animal. What fearful and amazing creations evolved! Refreshments were served attractively, and it might be added, eaten politely. Everyone helped with the cleanup, and the party was suddenly over.

What did the party accomplish? Fun and fellowship, of course. More than that, it gave the participants a sense of success in the responsibilities which they had undertaken. It developed a sense of competence in planning and working. The boy who did no more than take care of the familiar "Steal the Bacon" was a bigger person because of that act. The others listened to his directions and followed his leadership. That boy is better able and willing to take leadership in other activities.

What did the teacher learn? He saw his boys and girls in action. He saw their sense of humor and fair play. He saw how they responded to each other's leadership and how they carried through on jobs which they had undertaken. He saw a quiet youngster laugh aloud and speak more freely. He saw a noisy youngster kept in check by the group. He saw a response to orderliness and planning of which he had not thought his group capable. As for the boys and girls, they learned that good fun takes planning and is worth it. They saw their teacher in a new light—relaxed, enjoying their company, and laughing at their jokes.

Notice the general plan of the party. Atmosphere to greet people as they enter. A first activity that compels everyone to talk with his neighbors and mix around the room. A quick-tempo game involving everyone in close quarters. A sitting-down activity with opportunity to relax and watch as well as to participate. Next, action which includes everybody. Then a more quiet circle game with a secret element. Finally, an individual creative endeavor to cover the sometimes awkward pause just before refreshments are served.

This general plan of good mixing, then alternating active and quiet pursuits is suitable for all age groups. The necessity of planning *with* the participants is also true whether the party be for small children, youth, or adults.

Family Affairs

There is an important place for parties for the whole family in the program of the church school. We have learned to separate into age groups in order to meet the diversified needs of people in study and worship. On the other hand, we must do all we can to help unite the family.

In large churches, of course, it will be impractical to expect all families to attend one colossal gathering. Better fellowship and participation will be achieved by having several affairs for smaller groups. If space is no problem, these may all be held on the same night in different rooms in the church. Where assembly space is limited, it will be well to have groups of families invited on different nights. A problem of organization will be involved to make sure that many people share the planning and the leadership. Each group of families will need to have its own committee at work. The affairs will not be duplicate copies of one party, but each will be different in some respects.

The handling of large groups takes careful planning of details and strong leadership of the activities. A few moments of indecision or delay while the leaders consult or go over plans may be disastrous. From the time that the first few people enter until the refreshments are served, events must move swiftly and surely. While some events may be of the spectator nature, there must be provision for all to be active. In the chapter on "dramatic activities" there is an account of a family party following the birthday theme. The group was subdivided by birthday months, and each month prepared a skit and presented it for the others. Such organization into groups must be facilitated by clear directions and by signs designating places in which to meet.

Music is always useful at such parties. Everyone can sing if the songs are familiar and the leadership enthusiastic. The telling of a story in which everyone participates, as "The King with the Terrible Temper," is fun. Segments of the audience are designated by the storyteller to make certain noises or motions whenever the character they represent is named in the story. For another activity in the program, provide every family with newspaper and pins and the direction to dress one of the members of the family in the most unique costume the others can devise. Some families will dress the youngest, others the oldest. It makes no difference. At the end of the given time a parade will give opportunity for display of the family skill.

"Mother-daughter" and "father-son" dinners are regular affairs in some churches. Do we work hard enough at the program planning to guarantee that they will accomplish all that we want? Good food is extremely important, but it will

113

not necessarily develop the fellowship between father and son which is the purpose of the occasion. Try this: At one point in the program have all the fathers stand at their places and make simultaneous speeches on "Why My Boy Is the Best Son in the Room." Of course, pandemonium will result, and the only person hearing each speech will be the boy sitting next to the man. But that boy is the one who should hear his father speak on such a topic. And each father will have given expression to a few positive thoughts about his son. Reverse the procedure and let each boy speak simultaneously on "Why My Dad Is the Best One in This Room." The same action would of course be suitable for mothers and daughters.

Another way to help fellowship grow is to provide each parent and child with paper and pencil and ask them to list three things which they enjoy doing together. Collect the papers, without names, and have two or three readers share quickly what they see on the papers. Music and games are good for such an affair, though it is wise to avoid the demonstration of skill where comparisons will always be to someone's disadvantage.

All of this leads to the fairly obvious conclusion that other dinners and fellowship affairs ought to have more fun and fewer speeches. While speeches are the easiest way to solve the program problem, they are the least sociable of all ways of getting together. Take the anniversary dinner. We have accomplished ten, fifty, or even a hundred years of church life. And how do we celebrate? We have a dinner and invite all past ministers, superintendents, and other church dignitaries, introduce each one, and ask him to "say a few words."

With a little more effort we could highlight the past and point up the future in a program of music or skits that would interest young and old. The anniversary program should be

114

geared toward the young who are the future. Build the program around young Dick and Susan, who want to hear the story of the past, and help them to think of their contribution, which is now and in the future. We could still invite the dignitaries, and most of them would enjoy themselves just as much as if they had said a "few words."

Some churches have a fellowship hour after the Sunday-morning service once a month. No program is needed here but careful planning is important. How will we draw in those people who attend the morning worship but take part in no other activities? How can we promote fellowship among people who are not well acquainted? Do those who attend the social congregate only with their friends?

To make the social hour most effective we must study the membership and the attendance of the church. Beginning with those who attend worship but nothing else, we must organize for their inclusion. Certain persons are made the responsibility of each committee member. Throughout the month he seeks to make the acquaintance of these people. He makes a point of greeting them on Sunday morning. He gives them a special invitation to the fellowship hour, looks for them, and introduces them around. As the fellowship committee changes through the year, more and more of our members will be taking responsibility for a friendly atmosphere and for drawing others into active participation.

The same principles of planning apply to making the fellowship period of the youth meetings effective. People must be our concern. The question might be asked, "How much thought do we give to setting a friendly atmosphere at all our meetings and gatherings?" This is in line with the wider definition of recreation as that which relaxes tensions.

Clubs, Hobbies, and Crafts

The fact that more people have more leisure time is attested to in many ways, not the least conclusive of which is the greatly increased amount of money which Americans spend on materials for arts, crafts, and home repairs. "Do it yourself" is almost a national motto.

Some churches have hobby groups and craft clubs which meet regularly. The chief purpose for meeting is to engage in the activity with those who are like minded. There is at least one large church with more than twenty such groups meeting as classes every week. Others may exceed this. Where space, equipment, and employed personnel are available, the church can become a community center and extend its services to meet many unusual needs and interests. In the average church such groups for adults will be self-organized, depending on the drive of one or two enthusiasts of the activity.

What is it about making something yourself that is so good for the personality and self-esteem? We begin as two-year-olds when we set one block on top of another. See how the child chortles with delight and proceeds with the utmost care to build the blocks higher, higher. Soon the boy takes hammer and nails. The girl takes needle and sewing card. Both love the weaving loom and turn out myriads of pot holders. What adult has not been a recipient? All through elementary school interest is high in any art or craft activity.

In adolescence some of us find ourselves not so skilled or artistic as our neighbors. Rather than be embarrassed we drop such activity. Most of us never resume it. Yet there are a thousand crafts we have never tried! Many of them call for more patience than skill. All of them offer the reward of being able to say, "Why, yes, I made that myself."

Is there something of the great Creator in all of us? Do we

116

feel more important to life when we have made something with our hands, out of the thoughts of our minds? What a satisfaction to say, whether of a carving, a hooked rug, or a poem, "There! That was in my mind, and I have produced it."

These feelings are good. If there are those in our church who have no such opportunity, should we provide it? Think of the older folk especially. Here is one way of increasing our ministry to them. To seek out those who have hobbies and help them to share their interest with others would be a double ministry. Button and stamp collecting are two nationally organized hobbies which older folk especially enjoy. Painting has come into prominence because of some famous persons. Wood, metal, leather, and ceramics are high on the list of popular crafts. Do we know what hobbies the older people in our church already have? Just a listing of these, including names and addresses, might be a stimulus to others or aid them in finding persons with mutual interests.

Young people, of course, are also interested in hobbies and like to find others with whom they can share. While youth will want their own activity groups, an exhibit would be an excellent way to cut across age lines. A successful hobby fair can go far in developing family interest in a craft or hobby. Craft clubs are never at a loss for programs—they are too busy! They are enthusiastic, friendly, purposeful. They help to build happier, more resourceful people. As such they have a place in our program.

Team Sports

Many of our churches have basketball, softball, and other team sports. They participate in a church league where certain rules are usually enforced. There are restrictions on the age

117

and weight of the boys or girls involved, and membership and attendance qualifications to be met. The games are based on competition, and at the end of the season a league winner is announced. Teams which are not members of the league play invitation games with any other team which will meet them. At the end of the season they have their own record of wins and losses and points scored, but no competitive standing.

Judging again by objectives and accomplishments, there is much good in this activity. Assuming the older boy or man who coaches the team exemplifies the Christian character we wish the boys to achieve, they have an excellent opportunity to see and admire such character. The relation of coach to boys is a close and friendly one. In many situations the man becomes counselor and guide in personal problems. At least he has the opportunity to show his boys that he puts first things first, that playing fairly and with friendliness is more important than winning games. The times for practice and games give the boys that many more hours of fun and purposeful activity under the auspices of the church. And of course if the team is making a good record, there is the thrill of contributing to a successful enterprise.

On the other hand, some thoughtful questions need answering. Does the coach see himself as one of the corps of workers in the church school? Is he working toward the same objectives, though by a different path? Are there boys shut out from the play because of the higher value set on skilled players? What provision is made for these boys? What about the attendance requirement? Is Sunday-school attendance a price grudgingly paid for the privilege of playing ball? Is winning too important?

Many churches feel that we would do better to put our leadership and our energies into a broader sports and activity program within the church. The percentage of boys who can play on the team is too small. Emphasis on the team weakens the rest of the program and diverts our interest. The team, especially the winning team, gets the publicity and the laurels. "Leave that sort of team competition to the schools," some churches say. "Let us develop a program where everybody gets a chance and fun is more important that winning."

How do we go about it? Having talked over the function of sports and recreation in our commission on education, we appoint a person to assume organization responsibility. He will meet separately with the various age groups of young people. He will listen to their ideas, make suggestions, raise questions, and finally help them to work out a plan. He will also discuss with them the matter of leadership and solicit their help in securing the leaders on whom they have agreed. He will have the plans and leaders approved by the commission and will keep in touch with the groups after activities begin. Occasionally he will meet with the groups and their leaders to evaluate the program and increase its effectiveness.

How much can a small church do? Space rather than numbers is the chief limitation. But there is hardly a church that cannot find space for a dart board, shuffleboard court, and a ping-pong table. Where outdoor space is available, a net for volleyball, deck tennis, badminton, and other related games can be easily set up. Probably space can be found for a basketball net and backboard. And not too far away there may be a vacant lot or a playground where softball, dodge ball, and other outdoor events can be played.

Dancing

There are many churches which feel there is no place in our program for dancing. Some think that dancing is wrong at any time or place. Others feel that our program is rich in activities which contribute more to our fellowship than dancing would. There are some churches which exclude social dancing but develop a strong program of folk dancing and square dancing. Others say young people have always danced and always will, and we would rather have them dance in the church than in a tavern. Still others claim that dancing is one of the social graces and that we should help our young people to learn how to plan a dance so that everyone has a good time.

The matter is one for the local church to decide. Whichever way we decide, we have a responsibility following our decision. If we are of the group who will not allow dancing, then we must see that our program is rich enough to satisfy the needs of youth. If we are of the group which says, "Yes, youth may dance in this building," then we also have a responsibility to see that dancing is not simply an "easy way out" in party planning. When we have a dance, we must use it as an opportunity to help our young people to grow socially. Let us raise the question, "What can this dance help us to accomplish?" And let us not overlook the tremendous opportunity for developing world fellowship through folk dancing. We can draw closer to the people of another race or nation when we understand their music, their work songs, and their dances.

Finally

A guide has been prepared to help you to examine and evaluate the recreational program in your church. By checking what you have, leaving blank what you do not have, and adding additional activities, you should get a complete picture of your church at play. In the columns headed "Numbers" you will be interested in comparing the number of a particular

Study Your Church's Recreation Program

ACTIVITY	REGULARITY			PARTICIPATION			NUMBERS	
	Weekly	Monthly	Annual	Spectator	Partial	Full	In Church School *	Participating
Children's parties								
Youth parties								
Adult parties								
Family parties								
Father-son affairs								
Mother-daughter affairs								
Fellowship dinners								
Children's social hours								
Youth social hours								
Adult social hours								
Family social hours								
Hobby group								
Craft group								
Clubs								
Hikes								
Trips								
Concerts								
Team sports								
Other sports								
Other:								

* In the group eligible for the activity.

group who attend church school with the number who participate in a recreational activity in that group. For example, if one hundred youth are active in church school and only twenty attend a monthly social hour, you may want to study the planning for that social affair and the weaknesses in it. Checking this list may also help you to see blind spots in your church's recreation program.

The columns on participation simply ask: "Do the people who come merely watch as at a play? Is the program mostly spectator, with some participation? Is it an activity where everybody is up and doing?"

The comparison of numbers may help you in a very general way to see whether or not you are meeting the recreation needs of a sufficient number of your people.

A successful recreation program will be the product of group thought and action. Whether we are dealing with children, youth, or adults, they have the right to share in the planning. And when they plan, they think, they assume responsibility, and they grow. When we think about our recreation program, we will raise the question, "Why?" Why are we planning this activity? What do we hope to accomplish? In a successful recreation program the planning must be:

> Not for,
> > but with;
> Not what,
> > but why.

The church that plays together not only stays together, but it has greater fellowship among its members. It develops happier Christians who live and work more effectively.

CHAPTER VIII

THE USES OF DRAMA

DRAMATIZATION IS ONE OF THE EARLIEST OF CHILDHOOD activities. Through play children try to put themselves into a role. They try to be somebody other than themselves. Unconsciously they are trying to understand the world of people around them. The little girl who plays "mother" to her dolls is gaining some understanding of what it is to be a mother. The little boy who plays "father" is projecting himself into a role which may one day be his. Dressing up and acting are a means of entering into the larger world around us.

Dramatization is also an activity in which we develop our relationships with others. Young children "playing house" make demands of one another to meet the needs of the drama. In effect, they take leadership in their group and respond negatively or positively as members of a group. Older children and youth, for whom dramatization becomes something more than spontaneous play, respond to the co-operation demanded in such an enterprise in varying ways. Under skillful leadership a dramatic project becomes an opportunity for each person to make some significant contribution— whether it be in developing the play, acting, sewing, painting, getting properties, or doing any of the other jobs required.

The purpose of acting out the story in the kindergarten is that of making the story more real. We help the children to dramatize kindness, thinking by that means to bring kindness more clearly into focus. We forget that it is just as true of youth and adult groups that those who put themselves into another person grow in their understanding of that person.

Creative dramatics implies the use of imagination. We think our way into a situation or a character and work toward a solution or an understanding. In some cases this may mean writing a play or developing a play without writing it to express some idea or characterize some person or event. Or it may mean studying a play written by someone else and developing an understanding of the characters and situations which we find there. Creativity marks the difference between putting on a play and interpreting a play.

We enlarge our vision, develop our appreciations, and increase our power of thinking as we put ourselves in dramatic situations. How does this person think? Why does he think that way? What are his hopes and ambitions? What troubles him? As we ask such questions about the character whom we would portray, we get into his mind, we see through his eyes, and he takes on new meaning for us.

Another valuable outcome of creative dramatic activity is the self-assurance which develops as we live other roles. Perhaps we simply understand and appreciate our own background and abilities better as we look into other lives. Perhaps we thrill to the mosaic of differing personalities which the Creator has set within the human family. Perhaps we realize that there is within us all a deep well of power whose waters we rarely tap. Reaching out to interpret others, we strengthen our bonds with all humanity. Losing ourselves in creative expression, we stand more surely on our feet.

What better way to share an idea or a story than through a play? Here we have information, feeling, and action com-

124

bined to make their impact. Whether our purpose be to entertain, instruct, challenge, or to lead, we can reach our hearers through drama as through no other medium. The Church discovered this centuries ago and used drama for both teaching and preaching. Today in our church schools dramatic activity is used to share what we learn, to lift up ideas, and to aid in worship. In our times of recreation we use drama to draw groups together, to have fun, to entertain, and to relax.

Except for the occasional monologue and the one-man show, drama is group activity, and all that we have said in the preceding chapters applies to it. We are speaking of the two aspects of dramatic activity: (a) within the group for the group's use; (b) for sharing with another group in an audience situation. There are several aspects of such activity which we might examine.

Drama in the Fun Program

Who has not played charades? Whatever one thinks of the game, it is a part of both recreation and dramatics. We have a word, a phrase, or a saying which we must interpret by actions only to the rest of the group. However simple, unrehearsed, and ragged the performance may be, it is our own, and we are communicating an idea through its means. Church parties attended by the whole family are a natural occasion for charades and other forms of dramatic entertainment.

The values lie in the fact that everybody who wants to can get in the act, and that those who don't want to act can enjoy the entertainment as spectators. Take, for example, a party of 150 or more people of all ages. Their common interest at the moment is having fun at a party. After some good fellowship and laughter the director uses a rather simple device for breaking the mass into smaller units. He announces that this is a birthday party and that each person is to go to the month of his birth. Large signs direct the way and people wish each other "happy birthday" as they move. Each month-group is directed to develop and perform a skit showing one outstanding event which happened in that month, regardless of year.

Each group now has a problem with certain limits set. Each has a goal. Under pressure of action fellowship grows. Laughter is heard. Ingenuity produces costumes out of newspapers, scarfs, and anything else that may be at hand. In very short order time is called, and the skits are presented. No attempt is made at proclaiming a winner. All are given generous applause. And while the spirit of fun is still high, the director moves on to another phase of the party.

Fun? Yes. Creative and stimulating. We have been working with a group on a specific project. There has been opportunity for each person to contribute his ideas and share in the planning. Since this is a spontaneous grouping made without previous announcement, no one comes into the group with a preconceived idea of what the activity should be. In such a group one can observe many different roles at work. There will be the person who must have a book to turn to for ideas. Another person may try to dominate and direct the whole proceeding. Perhaps he has played that role with success before and he thinks of himself as the one who must get things done. Another role frequently seen in such groups is that of the clown. One member may shine as the "errand boy." He depends on others for ideas, but he achieves status by his ability to find props and equipment to carry out the ideas. There will be the quiet member whose chief contribution may be approval and praise which spurs on the others.

This type of activity is one of the best for helping a teacher to gain a clearer understanding of the needs and the abilities of her class. A department party in which each class has responsibility for preparing a skit spontaneously will provide rich opportunities not only for fellowship and fun, but also for deeper insight into the lives of those we teach.

In the Woman's Society

The woman's society, or guild, in almost every church has found the value of a dramatic presentation. The societies have used drama for many years, not only to press an appeal for missionary funds, but also to present information about the work and various fields of service. Sometimes the women ask a youth group to make such a presentation, but far greater values accrue to them when they plan and present their own drama. Here again they are thinking their way into a strange situation or a little-known character. They are participating in fellowship, thinking creatively, contributing to others, and growing through the group activity.

The brotherhood theme has found rich dramatic presentation by the women's groups, especially on the World Day of Prayer. Here all the pageantry of international costumes and flags are brought to give color to the idea of the world as being at one in prayer. And the languages of other nations, their customs and their aspirations woven into such a program lift the mind and heart and draw us together. We believe that there is one God, the Father of all, and we reach out to our brothers. Such is the power of a great idea capably presented by those who care.

In the Sunday-morning Class

Many a teacher has said, "I can't use drama in the Sunday school . . . I haven't a room for my class. Other classes are all around us. How could I let my class act out a play?"

But teachers in similar situations have used the dramatic method in teaching. The essential of drama is getting into the character of another person. For this no props, no scenery, no costumes are necessary. Action even can be dispensed with.

We are not speaking here of "putting on a play." Rather we speak of living the mind of the character in the play.

A group of intermediates questioned the story of the feeding of the multitude. They had read the account of the boy who offered his lunch to the Master and saw it distributed to feed thousands.

"How could he do it?" said one boy flatly. "I just don't think that's possible."

The teacher in preparation had thought through the same problem. She was aware of the difficulties involved in questioning a miracle. She knew the solution suggested by some that the boy's act of generosity had prompted others in the group until everyone shared and there was much left over. Would the boys and girls think that a suitable explanation? Was it better to say simply that there are some things we don't understand, but that with God all things are possible? Or was there perhaps a deeper lesson in the story for these questioning intermediates?

She thought there was, and she made ready to approach the matter through re-creating the boy in the minds of her students.

When the challenge came, the teacher waited. There were comments from the group about this and other miracles. Honest doubts and some fears were expressed. If you didn't believe the miracles, what could you believe?

At this point the teacher asked, "What is a miracle?"

That stumped the group momentarily. Then a girl said, "Well, it's something supernatural."

Another said, "It's something happening that you know couldn't happen."

"Suppose you took a radio to a primitive tribe of people and turned it on. Would they think that was a miracle?" asked the teacher.

The group agreed that they might. They decided that there might be cases where a miracle had some explanation which was unknown to those who saw it.

"We don't know everything," the teacher reminded them. "And I'm sure we don't know all the power of God. But I think there's another kind of miracle in the story we have read. Think about that boy and try to imagine his home and his day."

From what they knew of Palestine, the intermediates imagined the boy's home, his mother and father. Their teacher led them to wonder how it happened that this boy was in the crowd at Jesus' feet. They developed conversation that might have taken place in the boy's home that morning. They called the boy David, and the conversation ran something like this:

David: "Mother! Joel says that the Teacher is in our village. He says that everyone is going to listen to him on the hill outside the town. Joel's going. Mother, may I go? Can't you and Father go too?"

Father: "What teacher? What are you talking about, boy?"

David: "His name is Jesus. And already there are people leaving town to hear him. Joel heard him once and he says that there is no one like him. Can't we go, please?"

Father: "I have work to do. Other people can sit around. I must get to the shop."

David: "Please, Mother. I want so much to hear him. Can't you and I go?"

129

Mother: "Not I, Joel. I have too much work to do. But you may go if it means so much to you. It's a good day to be out-doors. I'll pack a lunch for you."

That ended scene 1. The group was satisfied as to why the boy was in the crowd and alone. When they got into scene 2, they made two important discoveries. In all that crowd the boy was on the front line, close enough to hand his lunch to Jesus. Then they discovered something else, even more star-tling to intermediates. Apparently the boy had been with the crowd all day. It was now evening. And the boy hadn't touched his lunch! What was more, when lunch was men-tioned, instead of feeling his hunger and eating, the boy gave his lunch to the Master.

"What a man he must have been!" said one boy, not ir-reverently.

They worked out a dialogue for the boy, the Master, and a disciple for scene 2. As they thought and as they talked, a new understanding of the personality of Jesus emerged. The physical miracle was unimportant to them now, so much greater was the impact of the man, not only on the boy of twenty centuries ago, but on themselves today.

Did this teacher need a private room for her class? Not at all. The crowded corner or the pew in the one-room church offer no barrier to creative dramatic thinking—unless the barrier be in the mind of the teacher.

Group thinking resulted in new and deeper convictions about Jesus. A sense of reality entered the picture that could not have been there had the teacher simply talked, expecting the group to listen. The teacher had prepared herself to stimulate and to guide thinking. She knew that if the boys and girls could put themselves in the place of this boy and get his feeling, the whole experience would come alive. It was a technique that was used often. Teacher and group were more at ease with it each time they approached a situation or a problem and tried to place themselves within the feelings of the characters involved.

In more spacious surroundings and with more time available, dramatic thinking can produce a play to be shared with others. No amount of space or production, however, will produce more significant results than this thinking and projecting of self into minds of long ago.

One of the most frequently dramatized stories in the Bible is that of the Good Samaritan. The teacher of young children learns by experience to begin the dramatization at the point where the man is lying in the road *after* the robbers have left. A group in a Pennsylvania mining camp vacation school very nearly did leave the victim half dead. It was one of this enthusiastic group who boomed out the innkeeper's response to frantic knocking on the door, "What you wake me up for? Why you knocking like that on my door at three o'clock in the morning?" Creative thinking!

Youth and adult groups have found it profitable to build the Samaritan story around modern situations in their own lives. According to one version, a woman was turned out of her rooming house and could find nowhere to go. Her church acquaintances shunned her, but a Jewish woman took her in and saw her through her trouble.

By such means an old teaching takes on new life. We begin to see the good Samaritans around us. We watch lest we also "pass by on the other side."

One warm summer morning during vacation church school a group of long-robed juniors filed silently out the church door. Each had a gaily colored Palestinian headdress, and a few carried staves. The tallest boy led the group to a shady place behind the church and solemnly sat down. Without a word the other juniors and their teachers, also robed, sat in a circle. Two boys brought twigs and logs and stacked these in the center of the ring.

"The night is too warm for a fire," the leader said. "Let us look up and enjoy the beauty of the stars."

After a moment one of the girls said, "The heavens declare the glory of God."

Another followed with these lines from Job:

> Stand still and consider the wonders of God.
> Do you know when God does his work,
> And causes the light of his cloud to shine?
> Do you know regarding the balancings of the cloud,
> The wonders of the one perfect in knowledge?
> (37:14-16 Amer. Trans.)

> Can you bind the chains of the Pleiades,
> Or loosen the girdle of Orion?
> Can you send forth Mazzaroth in its season,
> And lead forth the Bear with its satellites? (38:31-33.)

Then one of the teachers began to read from the Bible, "In the beginning God created the heaven and the earth." Slowly, majestically, she read the creation story. Each time that she read, "And God said," she paused, and the juniors in one voice responded with the words the ancient writer had set down as coming from God.

After this one of the juniors stood in the circle and in his own words told the story of Abraham's discovery that God wanted no sacrifice but obedience. When the storyteller sat down, the boy who had led the group out spoke the words of

Ps. 96:6-7 and gave a brief prayer of gratitude for the wonders of God known to men in all ages. When he had finished, he stood and the others followed. Silently he turned and led the way back into the church.

The dignity and serenity of the whole episode showed the depth of feeling which the juniors and their teachers had achieved. This was no spontaneous dramatization. It was the climax of many discussions and much preparation. The group had studied the customs of the ancient Hebrews, their dress, and their nomadic life. They had thought about the evening campfire and how the Hebrews would have shared their favorite stories in the few minutes of leisure before bedtime. The boys and girls had studied some of these stories and other songs and poems which the Hebrews might have used to express their feelings about God. They had made their robes and headdresses from old sheets and worked hard on their choral interpretation of the creation story. Finally the campfire program had been planned in detail and a leader chosen. Carrying out the plans was not only a climax to the study; it was an act of identification with men of old who knew God. And it was an act of worship as the boys and girls reached out toward God as they themselves might know him.

A good method of creating and sharing a drama where time and facilities are available is to record it on kodaslides or movie film. One group worked on the story of the Prodigal Son. They soon called it "The Story of the Forgiving Father," so greatly had their insight grown. They developed and practiced dialogue and finally wrote it exactly as they wanted it, with some narration. They studied biblical costume and dressed the characters for their play. After presenting the play once or twice, they decided to film it so that it might be shared with shut-ins. They recorded the dialogue and narration on a record. They found a good outdoor setting and took kodaslides of scenes to accompany the record. How grateful the shut-ins must have been who saw and heard the play in their own homes! And how satisfying to the young people to have created and shared so rich an experience!

Some Guidelines

To develop such a play, where do we begin? First, the story or the idea. In the case of the story of the Good Samaritan the events are clear. We will come later to the matter of selection of events. If it is an idea, such as kindness or brotherhood, around which we want to build a play, we think first of a situation.

We list the characters. As we think toward a play, there may be some of these we want to eliminate and others we wish to add. In the story of the boy and his lunch we added the mother and father. We eliminated all but one disciple.

Next we go over what happens and separate the events into scenes. We have as few scenes as possible. Again, we may eliminate scenes that are given in the story, such as the action of the robbers, and add others, such as the home scene between the boy and his parents.

Then we proceed to talk dialogue, letting various people take the parts. We give special attention to the opening line and the closing line of the play. Finally, if we are preparing our play for presentation, we select the persons who will be the characters. In some cases we will write out the dialogue, but in most cases this will be unnecessary and may even cause a stilted atmosphere.

If we are planning to use properties, costumes, and scenery, there may be jobs for persons not in the play. A scarf or headdress may help children to slip more easily into character.

With youth and adults this may cause self-consciousness. In vacation-church school with more time and personnel we may want to develop extensive scenery, props, and costumes.

When the play has been presented, there should be a time for evaluation centering around these questions: Did the audience get our idea? We presented the play in order to share a thought; did we do that effectively? What can we learn from this experience that will make our next play better?

Role Playing

In Chapter One we saw an example of role playing. The young-people's class studying a welfare problem projected that problem into the discussion by means of this technique. The young woman needing assistance and the welfare agent bound by regulations were thrown so sharply in relief that the group felt the problem emotionally and worked at a solution.

A class of women gained through role playing a new understanding of the sisters Mary and Martha and their dispute about the household tasks. The teacher directed each two women to assume the roles of the two sisters without moving from their seats, and all at once—one to be Mary, the other, Martha. As each Mary and Martha discussed her viewpoint about the problem, there were arguing, defense, pleading, and questioning. Each woman who was Mary tried to convince her partner of the rightness of her position. Each Martha did the same. After a few minutes the teacher quieted the group and asked the two sisters to reverse roles, to argue the opposite viewpoint. You would have thought a whole Palestinian village had gathered at the well!

Two or three of the couples had trouble with the technique. The teacher heard one woman saying, "Well, I think Martha

135

would have said this . . ." Another woman said, "I think Mary was right because . . ."

What was wrong? Were these women role playing? No! They were talking about a character instead of getting into the character. The technique of role-playing is not difficult to achieve. It takes imagination. And it is imagination which we must constantly use if we are to understand other people at all. When we learn to identify ourselves with others, at least to some extent, we see their problems and their motives. We think and feel as they do. We grow in our understanding of them and of their problems. We become larger persons mentally and spiritually.

In a workers' conference devoted to the matter of visiting pupils' homes, a superintendent asked his teachers to play the role of the boy who didn't come to Sunday school. What was his home situation? What did he think? What were his reasons for staying away? If he disliked Sunday school, why?

The group paired off, with one of each couple taking the role of the boy and the other of the teacher. Those who took the boy's part put up many convincing arguments for his staying away. After a few minutes the roles were reversed.

What was the result? These teachers gained new insight not only into the boy's thinking, but also into their own work. They saw themselves and their teaching through the boy's eyes.

What might not happen if we practiced role playing as we try to develop interracial understanding? Can a white youngster grow in his appreciation of his Negro brother when he puts himself in that boy's place? Can a Negro youth grow in understanding by putting himself in the role of a white boy? Not only do we need to see ourselves as others see us, but we need to see others as they see themselves.

A group of primary children began planning to send a box of supplies and clothing to a mission station. Their leader suggested that they imagine themselves as the children at the station. She helped them to think about the boys and girls, where they lived, what they played, and what their homes were like. She took the role of the missionary and led them to anticipate the box and what they would like to find in it. The children played their parts well. They saw the faraway children as persons. A friendly feeling toward them developed. When the planning session was resumed, there were thoughtful suggestions as to what should go into the box. And when the gifts were brought in, they showed the marks of careful selection. When the box was sent off, the givers went with the gifts in spirit.

In Worship

The function of worship is to direct the mind and the emotions toward God. The period of worship is a time for praise and prayer, for meditative thinking, for decision and commitment. Can dramatic activity aid in this? Or will it focus attention on the presentation and leave the worshipers with the spectator feeling, "That was a good program"?

One illustration may show how drama can serve the proper ends of worship.

A group of young adults planned a worship service on the theme, "The Call to Discipleship." They agreed that they needed to center attention on the personality of Jesus and thus open a way for group response to his call. They decided to present a brief scene in which Peter, James, and John would discuss their experiences of being called and their reactions to the Master. This would be followed by two or three challenging sentences with a meditative silence after each. At

137

the close they would have a responsive statement of dedication which would give the whole group opportunity for
expression.

Three men volunteered to prepare the scene. They read the
accounts of the calling and discussed the backgrounds of
Peter, James, and John. Then each assumed one of the personalities. They spent some time in silence, feeling their way
into the character. What would it mean to "leave all"? What
might they expect of this man who called them? What was
his program, his plan? What could they hope to accomplish
working with him?

When the men shared their feelings, all of them found
themselves coming back to the impact of personality which
Jesus must have made on the men he chose. They began to
feel personally this impact. Then they began shaping their
dialogue. The dialogue was not written down. The men made
notes on certain points that each would make and a general
plan as to how the conversation would open, develop, and
close.

When the dialogue was shared in worship, a miracle of
transformation occurred. The men said afterwards that they
felt as if they really were the three disciples and had actually
heard the Master. Members of the group later said they felt
transported in time and place, felt that they were sitting beside the sea feeling the presence of the unseen. The responsive statement at the close of the service was indeed an act of
dedication.

Drama achieved its function of being an aid to worship.
The idea got across to the group in such a way that performers
were forgotten. Could this focus on thought have been
achieved if the men had taken a play written by someone else
and presented it? It would have been much more difficult to

138

get their own feeling into printed words. It would have taken great actors to interpret such a play with power. These men, through thinking and planning together, had an experience which was theirs to share. What they said was authentic. It rang true in the hearers' ears. It carried conviction.

Here the distinction between sharing information and leading a group in worship is clear. A group studying the life of George Washington Carver, Paul, or Joseph may share that life in drama. A group studying a social problem may lift that problem to clearer understanding as they present it in a play. The woman's society may give information and appeal for funds through a wise use of drama. All these are good and worthy presentations. As spectators we listen, we watch, we learn, we may even be moved to respond.

Worshipers are not spectators. When we use drama as an aid to worship, a different quality enters into the sharing. The conviction must be felt that those who act are also worshipers. Feeling their consecration, we think and worship with them. The drama becomes a light, a path, a means of opening the door to larger vistas. We look not *at*, but *through* the drama, and we enter the presence of God.

There are many incidents, persons, and stories in the Bible which lend themselves well to the dramatic method. When we recall that learning follows thinking and that a major job of the teacher is to stimulate thinking, we readily see the values of creative dramatics. It is one thing to tell the story of Jesus as a boy asking questions in the temple. It is quite another thing to have a group of boys and girls imagine the kinds of questions he might have been asking.

The field for learning through drama is very rich for youth and adult groups. The older folk do not generally want to "get up and act," but they do find it stimulating and profitable to think their way into a long familiar Bible story or to imagine conversations that must have taken place. Ask a group of women at Easter time to see the events of Holy Week through Mary's eyes. Take the story of Zacchaeus and attempt to see what kind of person he had been and how he felt the influence of Jesus. When we can feel as he felt, we have a new experience of the power and love of Jesus.

The scene at the well in Samaria, the plotting of the Pharisees, the mental struggles of Judas, Paul writing a letter, Job fighting an idea, Nehemiah restoring a wall and a people, all these are episodes fraught with possibilities for creative adults.

The chief danger in using the dramatic method is its very realism. Particularly with children's groups the teacher must use care in selecting material. You will notice in the junior-campfire scene related earlier that the story of Abraham and Isaac was told, not acted. The story of the Crucifixion, while it might be used powerfully with adults, is beyond the emotional maturity of children insofar as trying to feel it and re-create it through drama is concerned.

Three guidelines for the teacher to keep in mind might be: (a) Is there a truth in this story or event which has special significance for my class? (b) Will re-creating the scene dramatically in the minds of the class be the best means of making the teaching come alive? (c) Will this activity provide opportunity for creative thinking and planning by the group?

CHAPTER IX

GROUP EXPERIENCE IN CHORAL SPEAKING

TO ONE WHO CANNOT SING BEAUTIFULLY THE DISCOVERY OF choral speaking is an opening door. To anyone who loves great literature, the sound of words, and the noble expression of fine thought, choral speaking offers a new experience in understanding and enjoyment.

With the exception of melody choral speaking involves the use of every technique known to the singing choir, plus the additional freedom that comes from not being bound by the measures of printed music. There is opportunity for creative thinking about the passage to be interpreted chorally. Rich hidden meanings in the words come out as we try first one interpretation and then another.

A group of juniors was preparing the Christmas story for choral speaking as their part in a Christmas service. When they came to the verse, "And when they had opened their treasures, they presented unto him gifts," there was long discussion as to how the words should be said. Some felt that the word to be emphasized most was "him" since the gifts were being made to the Christ child. One boy said, "No, the important thing is the gifts." Other words in the line were suggested as being most important. Finally the

141

sentence was spoken in every different way possible. When emphasis was put on the word "treasures," a new understanding came over the group. One of the children summed up the feeling: "They didn't give him their leftovers or something they didn't want. They brought their treasures!" The group agreed that this was the way they understood the line and wanted to say it.

The important thing here is that the leader, while he had thought deeply about the passage, did not come to the group with a preconceived idea that it would go best with one particular emphasis. He had given the passage enough thought to be aware of many feelings and possibilities of interpretation. Yet he wanted primarily to involve the group in the passage to the extent that it would take on deeper meaning for them. The interpretation must be theirs, not his. As the group shared ideas, there was good thinking. The more people, the richer the interpretation.

Use choral speaking for a psalm or poem which your group has written. The piece will take on deeper meaning, even for those who shared in the writing. Speaking it chorally, the group will be able to share their thoughts with others in the beautiful setting that good words deserve. Some young people wrote a psalm of Thanksgiving, spending much time in thought about what gave them greatest cause for giving thanks. The psalm took the form of a litany. They named homes, country, friends, church, memories, learning, and the example of great leaders as the things for which they were most thankful. A sentence or two was written about each idea. After each idea a refrain followed, "We give thee thanks, O Lord." In sharing the litany with a larger group, half the young people spoke the idea. The whole group joined in on the response. On the next idea the other half spoke. Again the whole group joined in the response. So it went through the whole litany, giving variety and depth to the words.

Choral speaking also has the value of letting the shy person participate freely. Speaking with others, he loses the fright of his own voice. As he gains confidence, he finds a fullness in his voice that he had not known he possessed. He may even find himself expressing his ideas more easily alone. He has at least had the happy experience of contributing his voice to help make some expression more beautiful, more meaningful.

For junior-high-school people choral speaking is especially helpful in a practical way. It gives them the opportunity to try out the new, wider range of their voices without being subject to embarrassment. To speak as softly as possible, and then again with great volume, to speak in a voice as low deep down as a well, or again in a voice as light as a trembling summer breeze, helps a boy or girl to find new confidence in his voice and to develop its use. Choral-speaking youngsters do not grow up to become nasal-voiced adults. A pleasant and a powerful voice is a great asset. Practice, confidence, and enjoyment in the use of the voice contribute to this very practical goal.

A basic question about choral speaking is this: How does the untrained leader who wants to use this technique with his group begin? The answer is simply: *Think* and begin.

Start your group off with a well-known nursery rhyme. Adults have as much fun as children saying "Humpty-Dumpty sat on a wall." Start your group on the rhyme and then listen as they speak. Get some fun and laughter into the experience. Nothing frees and unites a group so quickly as laughter. Try another nursery rhyme, and this time mark the tempo with your hand, keeping the voices together. Take "Little Jack Horner." After the group has said the rhyme once, ask individuals to give some different inflections to the last line, "What a good boy am I." The boy can sound like anything from a prig to a clown depending on how the words are said.

To get a different experience, use the verse, "Pussy cat, pussy cat, where have you been?" Divide the group into two parts without any attempt at locating voices. Let one group ask the questions and the other group answer. Still keep the experience one of fun. No dull flat voices saying, "I've been to London to see the queen," but "*I've* been to London, to see the *queen.*"

Then try "Jack Be Nimble." Let one group say the first line, the second part the next line, and the whole group the final line, "Jack jump over the candlestick." Say the verse very fast without any break in the rhythm. It is not as easy as it sounds. If you are speaking with primary children, let them jump, still in rhythm, on the next beat after candlestick.

So you have begun. And what have you accomplished? You have led your group in having fun doing something together. Everyone has taken part. Each one has discovered and used his voice with the others. There has been a discipline within the group as each tries to stay with the rhythm. You have given them experience with unison and two-part speaking. And you have given them opportunity to try their own interpretations of the ways in which familiar words may be said. Also you have given yourself some experience, perhaps some pleasure and some confidence in choral-speaking leadership.

When you are ready for serious work with your group, you will want to arrange your speaking choir by voice. Speaking voices and singing voices do not always correspond. A woman may be able to sing notes very low on the scale and yet have what we call a "light" speaking voice. A little practice in listening will enable the leader to group the choir in many arrangements. For two-part work with adults there will usually be the men's voices in one group and the women's in another. But there will be exceptions. Some women's voices will be heavier than some men's. With very young children there will be little difference in the voices of most. It is hardest to group the junior- and senior-high-school ages. And there will be need for constant regrouping since the voices are developing and changing. Most choral work for this group, and indeed for older and younger groups as well, will fall easily into a three-part division: high, or light, voices; medium voices; and low, or dark, voices. There will occasionally be work in which you will want a cumulative effect, starting with a very few voices, adding a few more, then more and more until a climax is reached. This, added to volume control, can give a startling effect.

Rhythm is essential to effective speaking, but it can be a pitfall. All too often we have heard unskilled recitations of poetry in a sing-song manner. The beat of the poem has been strictly adhered to, but true rhythm is lacking. It is particularly necessary to help children to see the complete thought in a poem, never reading line by line. Here again the interpretation of meaning by the group helps to subdue the rhythm to its proper place of undercurrent.

In the matters of tone, volume, and breathing, little can be said that common sense will not readily support. Good posture, for example, leads to better speaking. Deep breathing produces a better tone of voice. A rounded mouth opening produces a rounder tone than a thin flat opening of the lips. Good diction involves the use of many muscles. Very loud and very soft speaking require additional attention to diction. And it is most important that loud speaking come from deep within the diaphragm.

In all of these matters nothing will take the place of thoughtful practice and experimentation. If your group is thinking and experimenting with you, together you will achieve skill in speaking and pleasure in using this method of interpreting and sharing fine writing.

Use choral speaking for a psalm and see how the words take on new meaning. An adult group studying the first psalm this way was delighted with the discovery of the word progression of "walk," "stand," and "sit." In changing from light to dark voices, they brought out the contrast between the good man and the wicked. Thinking about how the words should be spoken led to thinking about the meaning of the psalm.

Many of the psalms are meant to be used antiphonally or as litanies. They lend themselves so well to this treatment that one is tempted to speak them as they appear. Our purpose, however, is to stimulate thinking as well as to speak the passage beautifully. Without drawing out discussion too far, the leader must be sure that everyone has opportunity to suggest his interpretation of the piece. Then the emphasis which most people agree on is adopted and the interpretation is set.

The psalms are not the only portions of the Bible which can be used effectively in choral speaking, but they will help us to illustrate some of the wide variety which can be obtained through this medium.

A good example of antiphonal work is Psalm 24. The first two verses are a statement of creation and might be spoken in unison by all voices. Then come the questions and answers. Through several readings of the psalm, the group would have to decide whether the light voices or the dark voices should ask the questions. The group may feel that since there is more power of assertion in the answers, the dark voices should take this part. Another approach to this psalm would be to have a light group, a dark group, and a solo voice. In this case the light group and the dark group together could affirm the opening stanzas and the solo voice ask the questions. After the first question the light voices might answer alone. After the second question in vs. 7 the dark voices might answer alone. And after the final question both groups could join together in the strongest affirmation with which the psalm ends.

Psalm 46 is a good example of contrasts. It moves from the strength of God in the roaring earthquakes to the river of vs. 4, whose streams make glad the city of God. Then the psalm builds up again to a climax in vs. 7. Verses 8-10 introduce a mood of quiet and peace, ending with the line, "Be still, and know that I am God." This is a line which a group might want to whisper. The last two lines of the psalm would undoubtedly be spoken with all the strength of the combined voices of the group.

Psalm 136 offers the interesting possibility of an undercurrent refrain throughout the song. From vs. 2 to vs. 25 there is not one period or break in the psalm. Much of its beauty and movement is lost by the somewhat monotonous repetition of the refrain, "For his kindness is everlasting." If a group can feel the pulse of this refrain and put the opposing lines into that same rhythm, they can maintain a continuous speaking of both parts at the same time. Let the deep voices take the refrain and speak it softly but with definitely marked rhythm. The lighter voices take the first line of each verse, but after vs. 1 let them begin speaking immediately after "For his kindness." The dark voices maintain a continuous flow of the refrain, with the light voices speaking over them and always coming in at the same place. Finally at the conclusion of the psalm the dark voices have one full line of refrain after the light voices finish.

Psalm 148 is one which boys and girls like to speak chorally because of its closeness to Francis of Assisi's "Canticle of the Sun." And Psalm 150 offers an excellent opportunity for a study of the musical instruments of the Hebrews. Boys and girls like to make its "Hallelujah" ring and speak the first two and one-half verses with full strength. Usually they see a contrast coming in the line about the lyre and lute. They like to take this line softly and build gradually back to full strength for the crashing cymbals and the final "Hallelujah."

The Christmas story, with its angel's voice, Mary's song, and Simeon's prayer, gives ample opportunity for the use of solo voices. The Palm Sunday story with its "Hosannahs" is another of the passages which reads particularly well chorally. Throughout the Old Testament there are songs and poems which a group used to choral speaking would want to interpret. A class or department studying ideas of God in the Old Testament would find choral speaking of selected passages an excellent way to tie their study together and enrich it. And there are many passages in the words of Jesus and in the writings of Paul which ought to be in our possession. A sharp and living challenge to any group which prepares it for choral speaking is I Cor. 13.

The important thing always is that the thinking and the interpreting shall be done by the group. If the leader says, "Do it this way," the effect is much the same as putting on a play. If we are trying to make the Bible come alive, to get

148

inside it, and to get it inside us, the thinking and the interpretation must grow within ourselves. We find help in sharing the thoughts of a group and the inspiration of a good teacher, but the thoughts we hold and live by must be our own.

A group of more than a hundred young adults at a conference had come together after a busy day of discussion and speeches for a time of relaxing and enjoying choral speaking. Few had ever participated in the art. The leader used "Humpty Dumpty" to break the ice and give the group a sense of togetherness. The ice was effectively broken when one of the group suggested the addition of the words "Poor Humpty" at the end of the rhyme.

Next a poem about the wind gave everyone a chance to blow off steam. The poem was done in two parts, one part speaking the poem while the other part gave a whistling, rustling undercurrent of wind effect. Of course the poem was done a second time with the parts changed so that everyone had a chance at being the wind! Someone suggested that the wind ought to begin blowing before the words began and that both should reach a peak of volume in the middle of the poem, then die away, with the sighing of the wind continuing for a second at the close of the poem. The effect was far different from anything the leader had anticipated. It was an immediate success. The group was functioning; it was creative; it was having a wonderful time.

James Weldon Johnson's sermon-poem, "The Creation," had been used at the conference earlier in the day. Parts of this were taken by the group and interpreted chorally. Small parts of it were used, so there was no need to have anything written. Papers or blackboard would have been artificial,

149

and they would certainly have detracted from the air of relaxation.

One sentence that the deep-voiced men enjoyed especially was:

> Darkness covered everything,
> Blacker than a hundred midnights
> Down in a cypress swamp.[1]

No cypress swamp was ever further down than that one! The contrast of the next line was carried by the lightest voices: "Then God smiled."

A few lines of very fast-running words loosened any remaining tight muscle. When the hour was up, the group had three small parts of the poem interpreted and spoken to their satisfaction. They also had a refrain that fitted in after several sections of the poem. As a conclusion to the hour the leader spoke the poem, drawing the group in on the parts that had been practiced. It was obvious that the group had found relaxation and pleasure in an hour thus spent.

In another session the group turned to the majestic poem of creation found in Gen. 1. Parts of this were taken by the group and interpreted chorally. Small parts of it were used, so there was no need to have anything written. Only the leader and the solo voices had the words before them.

The rhythm of movement was appreciated as the group saw how the poem was divided into parts by the words, "Evening came and morning came, making the first day." They practiced this line to get just the right shading of pause and rest. They saw how each new day and act of creation began with the words, "And God said." One of the men who

---

[1] Used by permission of The Viking Press, New York.

had a particularly good voice was chosen to speak the words attributed to God.

Following each of God's utterances the group saw the pattern of the words, "And it was so. . . . And God saw that it was good." They worked on these lines and selected an individual to read the detailed parts about each day's creation. When they came to vs. 27, where God created man in his own image, they decided to speak this verse in unison rather than solo because of its significance. Similarly, they all spoke the summarizing vs. 31, where God saw all that he had created. A solo voice read the next three verses which conclude the story.

At this point there was some dissatisfaction. Many in the group felt that there should be a concluding line spoken in unison, yet the last line of the poem did not quite meet the need they felt. Several lines were suggested and tried, such as, "God created everything good," "God is the creator of all," and "In the beginning God created the heavens and the earth."

One young woman spoke excitedly after this last trial: "The point is that God is the beginning of everything. We don't all agree on the details of creation, but we do agree that God is the will and purpose and guide in the universe. So why not end the poem simply with the first four words, 'In the beginning God'?"

The group tried the phrase very slowly and quietly with a long pause before the last word. Agreement was unanimous. The choral speaking had ceased to be merely the beautiful rendering of a great poem. In those four words the group had found an affirmation and a conviction. They had found a kinship with the ancient writer. There might be questions

151

among the scientific as to the details of creation, but a firm unity of fundamental belief filled the group.

That evening at vespers, sitting on the hillside and watching the glow of fading sunset, the group spoke the poem in worship. It was an act of reverent appreciation and dedication. An ancient truth had taken on new life.

Aside from its value for pleasure, its value for developing voices and confidence, and its value for reading more deeply into the meanings of great writing, choral speaking has its finest use in the service of worship. Think of the effect of having the psalms or some other poetic passage of scripture read chorally on a Sunday morning! Here also is an excellent way for the superintendent to bring in class participation in the departmental worship service. The Christmas story and litanies of Thanksgiving, as we have already seen, lend themselves very well to choral interpretation. Dramatic services of worship can also make effective use of the speaking choir.

A group of intermediates developed such a service at the conclusion of a study of the prophets. The service was extremely simple but powerful in its effect of drawing together the great thoughts of these men. The effect was similar to that of John Sargent's frieze. One after another the prophets appeared before the group in characteristic dress and pose. A spokesman gave a sentence or two about each one and his teaching. A choir speaking in the background then gave a verse or two that was most familiar from the prophet's writing. The dignity of the young people, the quality of their expression, left no doubt that their best thinking and planning had gone into this summary and sharing of their studies.

A final word about choral speaking and memorization. The juniors referred to earlier prepared the entire Christmas story, combined from Matthew and Luke, but with the genealogies and a few verses omitted. The story took one complete page, single spaced. When the papers were handed out at the first meeting, a cry of dismay arose from the group. "Do we have to memorize all this?"

The leader said, "No, you don't have to," and went on to the interpretation of the material. It was the juniors' interpretation that was used all the way through, just as we have seen with the word "treasures." There were six sessions spent in preparing the passage for the Christmas service. At the fourth session two of the girls announced, "We don't need our papers." The leader commended them and went on with the practice. She noticed that very few were using their papers. At the beginning of the fifth session one of the boys said, "Don't let's use papers. I think we do better without them."

Memorization? Yes! With understanding, appreciation, and use. Choral speaking gives all three with the additional values of fun and fellowship.

Dramatization and choral speaking are two of the finest techniques which a creative teacher can use. They are not limited to any age group or space requirements. Even in crowded quarters choral speaking can be done in whispers and will cause less confusion than a loud-spoken teacher. And certainly in crowded situations where the making of charts, posters, dioramas, time lines, and the like may be impossible, creative dramatic thinking offers one of the best means of achieving group participation. So long as we think of the "lesson" as something within the teacher or the book to be transferred to the pupil, we will be content with teachers who tell and with classes who quietly "behave." When we realize that learning must be active on the part of the learner, that he grows by his own thought and study and experience, we see the importance of stimulating thought and expression.

Creative dramatics and choral speaking are two very rewarding forms of activity for a group. Skill in these techniques comes like skill in anything else—through thoughtful practice and evaluation. Even a first attempt, however, can be very satisfying when a group has developed through shared thinking a new height of understanding and expression.

Good choral speaking or creative dramatics is a happy experience. Minds are united for interpretation. The group shares in planning action. There are many opportunities for group decision. The accomplishment, whether it be entirely within the group or shared with others, is significant to the participants. They have a sense of success, a sense of belonging to an effective group.

CHAPTER X

TOWARD MORE EFFECTIVE GROUPS

THE WORK OF CHRISTIAN EDUCATION IN THE LOCAL CHURCH is the responsibility of many people. All types of activities are included in the Christian nurture of children, youth, and adults. Leaders of recreational activities, choirs, clubs, adult organizations, and members of church boards and committees all have an important part to play in guiding religious growth. No longer can we say that the Sunday-school teachers alone have the job of Christian education.

The new concept of education sees learning in terms of the growth of persons—growth that is moral, spiritual, social, and intellectual. There is a new understanding of the importance of human relations, of the need for learning to live together, of the necessity for helping individuals to become active participants in the society of which they are a part. When we check our accomplishments in the church by the framework of objectives set forth in Chapter Two, we take a new look at persons and at our task. We recognize that it is not enough to ask, "Does he know his Bible?" but rather, "How well is he learning to live the truths of the Bible?" To this question the recreation leader may have a more valid answer than the Sunday-school teacher. When

155

all the workers in a church have a sense of common purpose and community of effort, each is bolstered and challenged by the others.

In the Church-school Staff

It is at this point that the minister, the director of Christian education, the church-school superintendent has a concern for developing a group consciousness on the part of all those who work in the program of the church. The development of that fellowship of co-laborers goes right back to the beginnings of Christianity. Paul wrote to his fellow workers reminding them that while there were diverse gifts and jobs, there was one body of which all were a part. It is this bond of common endeavor which the leader in the church school must seek to establish among all those who work with him in Christian education. We will speak of this leader here as the church-school superintendent since he is the one officially designated in most churches by the minister, the church board, or the commission on education to organize, supervise, and develop the educational work of the church.

Where does the superintendent begin to develop this "we-feeling" on the part of his workers?

His job in this respect, with relation to the corps of workers, is very similar to that of the class teacher or club leader. He can begin to build a good group only by knowing each individual and developing a good personal relationship with him. The superintendent must be concerned first with persons. He must know every worker by name and by family. When he first takes up the job as superintendent, he can profit greatly by a series of home visitations to discuss the church school with each of his co-workers. In a very large staff he may have to confine his home visits to the heads of departments and other special leaders such as the choir director, recreation leader, and the president of the woman's organization. By going to these persons individually, he is in effect saying, "You are important to this work." As he discusses problems, opportunities, and as he listens, he will gain not only in ideas but also in support from each person he visits.

Along with his personal interest in each worker the superintendent must try to develop among the workers a friendly interest in each other. As he listens, he may become aware of the tensions between individuals. He becomes more alert to opportunities for helping these individuals to draw together. He helps each one to a greater sense of worth in what he is doing, and at the same time tries to develop appreciation for the work of the other. In informal contacts and at workers' conferences he tries to help leaders to become better acquainted with each other. He makes provision in meetings for some fun and laughter so that his co-workers will enjoy being together.

He begins to build the group fellowship also by leading the workers into a consideration of objectives or purposes. A meeting set up for discussion of this topic may start out with an empty silence. The superintendent may need to have printed materials at hand to stimulate thinking. The National Council of Churches and the general boards of denominations, as well as the church-school magazines and lesson materials, have excellent statements about both general and specific objectives. There are visual aids in the form of sound filmstrips available from these same sources which the superintendent may use to help stimulate thinking. As in all the experiences related thus far, however, the essential element is that the group shall make its own statement of objectives. To adopt a formula prepared by another group, no matter how good, never quite puts a group on record with the same conviction as when the members develop their own.

The statement of goals becomes a frame of reference on the basis of which the superintendent can subsequently lead his group in evaluating what program and emphases they have and in planning what action they wish to take. Here again, planning by the group makes for a sense of "our" plans. The superintendent who tells his group what he wants them to do will sometimes get co-operation, but he has denied the group the right to give of their own best thinking. The are not likely to be as good as plans made by a concerned group thinking together. Group planning develops a greater measure of group responsibility.

Evaluation is essential if a group of leaders is to obtain maximum benefit from working together. Evaluation is the process of examining our work and our accomplishments, weighing their strengths and weaknesses, consolidating our gains, and learning from our failures. In a sense, we "set a value" on what we have done when we evaluate. The superintendent who leads his staff in this process will use much the same questions as were suggested for the class teacher or group leader in Chapter Four. Planning for further action grows out of evaluation.

One other step is involved in the development of group consciousness and endeavor on the part of a church-school staff. This is the matter of leading workers into an ever deepening commitment to the fellowship in Christ and joyful response to the will of God. Church-school leadership begins with following, not leading. We become better leaders as we seek to become better followers. As we deepen the wells of our own spiritual experience and conviction, we have that much more to give to others. We may assume that the superintendent and his workers were all drawn into Christian service because of a commitment to Christ. We cannot assume that the service in itself will keep the fires of the spirit glowing. One of the major responsibilities of the superintendent is to make provision for inspiration, challenge, and the expression of rededication. A group of people consecrating themselves together and caring about each other will help each individual in his resolve. It is the principle of putting oneself on record with a group of friends. The strength of the group is added to the strength of the person, just as the conviction of each person lifts the group to higher goals than one individual alone would attempt.

This is the same principle that groups of Christians find valid when they meet together for prayer. They find power in group prayer which can bring about change in themselves and in others. There is a plus quality which makes the strength of the group greater than the total of the individual strengths of the members.

When a group of church-school leaders meets together in mutual concern and shared consecration, they find power released among them that makes it literally possible to "do all things through Christ." When a group operates at this level, both the group and all individuals in it are lifted above the best they had ever contemplated or experienced before. Suddenly they realize there is no need either for weariness in well-doing or for failure. "Power from on high" becomes a living truth.

In the Leadership Education Class

When morale is high and consecration deep, leaders want to grow. A major problem in Christian education is that of making leadership classes attractive and effective. The principles of group dynamics can help us at this point. The superintendent, the committee, or the instructor who plans a course for leaders will find their work more successful if they apply to it the techniques which we have been studying.

For many years church-school workers have been attending leadership training classes both in the local church and in community schools. Some of these classes have effected significant changes in the approach and the techniques of the participants. Many a church-school leader, however, has attended one class or a long series of classes without really learning how to do a better job of teaching. Sometimes the difficulty is a closed mind on the part of the student. Can such minds be opened? Sometimes the difficulty lies with the technique of the instructor who, paradoxically, tells people how to teach. He may even tell them that learning is an active process, that people learn very little, if at all, by listening. And he expects them to learn this by listening to him! Can instructors of leadership classes take their own teachings seriously? Sometimes the block to learning is a sense of inferiority on the part of a student whose schooling may be limited. Can such a student be freed for learning? Finally, the difficulty may be one of too great a chasm between desired perfection and known imperfection. The goal set by the instructor in the class may be so far removed from the conditions with which the student has to work that the result may be complete frustration or rejection. Can teaching be more nearly in line with the learner's present understanding and problems?

There are five guidelines which may help to make the process of leadership education more effective. These guidelines are

160

based on the same fundamentals of group life and learning that apply to all other group activities in the church school.

1. *Acceptance.* The student and his ideas must be accepted as having worth. No ridicule or blame can be attached to the limited understanding, the concepts, or the methods of the teacher who enters a leadership education class seeking help. The instructor of the class must attain the point of view that every student in the class is as he is because of experiences or limitations which he has in his background. Help must be given in terms of that background, the felt needs, and the abilities of the student. The instructor must challenge the advanced and walk slowly with the limited. Advanced or limited, the student must feel accepted if he is to be ready to grow.

2. *Fellowship.* The student must be surrounded with a sense of fellowship and belonging. If in the class the students have a sense of common goal, that all are trying to help others grow in love of God and Christian living, there will be a greater readiness to listen to differences in approach or method. Each student must have a feeling that others are glad that he is present and that he has something to give as well as receive. There must be a friendliness felt within the group and between the leader and each member of the group. People who like us are ready to learn from us. A friendly atmosphere produces a positive and open frame of mind.

3. *Purpose.* There must be within each person in the leadership class a sense of worth, purpose, and goal. In most cases the desire to reach a goal brings out a need for help. Where the group together is facing a worthy purpose and asking how they shall attain it and what are the problems that prevent attainment, the individual is freed to some

161

extent to express his feelings of need. Visits, visual aids, and discussions may help to develop a sense of purpose and goal. They may also increase the student's range of experience so that needs may be seen to exist where they were not realized before. It is important in the attempt to help people grow to assist them to verbalize their problems, defining them and seeing of just what elements they consist. Goals must be in terms of the immediate and attainable as well as the long-range objectives. Learning that is goal directed is effective learning. The work of a class or group that is directed toward problem solving or desired objectives will call forth the best co-operative endeavor. When goals become important, we work together purposefully.

4. Involvement. Students must be involved emotionally and practically in the problems and opportunities brought into the class. The problems which are discussed must be seen as their own problems. Within the area of a course it must be the students' problems which are the focus. Small groups within the class for discussion, study, or for role playing help to involve the students. They may work on rearranging the room for better teaching, scraping and painting, making or mending. They may be involved in making home visits along with a class discussion of home visits. Instead of looking at and talking about songs, the students should sing them. The leadership class or conference will be an active effort, physically and emotionally as well as mentally, if it is to achieve maximum benefit. This involvement will never be mere busy work and sociability. It will be rich in content and directed toward the achievement of goals set by the student.

5. Continuance. The fellowship built up during the learning experience must continue. The leadership class will be most effective if it is job related. This is the value of conducting such classes within the local church and under local leadership. The instructor is likely to be more familiar with the problems his students will face. He is available for follow-up work as the students begin to put ideas into practice. He should be looked on by all the workers as "one of us," a regular member of the staff, available for teaching groups of workers or counseling individuals. Thus the experience in leadership education is not isolated, but a vital ongoing part of being one of the group of leaders in the church.

It is essential that instructors in leadership classes be skilled in discussion leadership and in the ability to stimulate thinking. This is prerequisite. The guidelines enumerated here take the leadership class beyond good discussion and point it more definitely toward a group learning experience which produces change.

In the Christian Family

There is another area of Christian fellowship in which the techniques of group work are being used today as never before. This is the Christian family. As greater emphasis is placed on Christian family life, conferences are being held throughout the land for study of new approaches to living together in families. The family is the first group to which most people belong. Scarcely more than a generation ago families, however loving, were based on the autocratic principle that father is the head of the household and his word is law. Next to father in authority came mother. Children had few rights and little recognition.

The family has changed! After a period of vacillation the family today is emerging as a fellowship where each member has both rights and responsibilities. The family council has developed as a meeting ground where family problems may be discussed by the whole family and where group decisions are made. Daily family worship is in action once more, but in new guise. Materials for this devotional time are planned with the interests and needs of children in mind. Prayer may be made by any member, and Bible readings may be selected co-operatively and sometimes read by the child or youth in the family.

The family has learned to talk together and to play together. Family vacations are times for family fun. Budgets and finances are discussed with a greater degree of freedom than ever before. Jobs are shared on a basis of understanding our mutual responsibilities. After a period of grave problems and near disintegration, families are being solidified again as the primary group to which anyone belongs. This strengthened family, like the church-school group, is built on a uniting of minds, a desire to grow, shared planning, group decision, concern for each individual, regularity, action, and evaluation. How can the church better strengthen Christian families than by giving the members experience in groups that function by these same principles?

In Today's World

One final word should be said about the importance of a vital group relationship to the individual in today's world. The world we live in has become so far removed from the individual citizen's personal responsibility that a feeling of hopeless inertia has claimed many who otherwise would work untiringly for civic betterment and good international relations. One is so overwhelmed by the millions of this and the billions of that, that as an individual, he feels insignificant and frustrated. Urged to vote, he says, "Why should I?

What difference does my vote make?" Man is in a new, modern dilemma. Through television, radio, and reading, and through his own personal travels and long-distance phone calls, he is in closer touch with the whole world than man has ever been. Yet the vast array of statistics thrown at him as well as the largely spectator nature of his knowledge make him feel utterly impotent as far as having any effect on his world is concerned.

It is in such a world as this that small, face-to-face groups are taking on great significance. The American town hall is returning. It is returning in labor unions, in women's clubs, in farm organizations, and civic groups. More than anywhere else the town hall is returning in our schools—elementary as well as junior- and senior-high schools. In classes and groups of all kinds the art of discussion is being practiced by leaders who study discussion technique and group-work methods. In the schools children and youth are learning how to be panel moderators and discussion leaders. Americans by the millions are learning to reason together. Our world became so big that we nearly got lost in it. Almost we forgot that it is persons, individual persons, who count.

If we believe in democracy, we will practice democracy. In a democracy everyone counts and everyone has responsibility. Everyone is concerned for the good of all. This attitude we do not learn easily. Schools and youth groups attempt to teach it by giving boys and girls experiences in self-government and committee responsibilities and by teaching them to think accurately. If democracy is to flourish, everyone needs to have a sense of belonging, a sense that he counts for something, and that he is a contributing member. There is no other way in which our millions of citizens can feel this except as they find some success and satisfaction in group activity.

Will the Church lead the way today in concern for others and in the long crusade for better government and better communities? Will the Church inspire and prepare men and women to live at their best as Christians in the nation? Will the Church challenge what is evil and uphold what is good? Then the Church must give children, youth, and adults opportunities within its doors for thinking and living as Christians in the world. It must teach them to join their thoughts in the search for truth. It must lead them to care within the small, friendly group and must challenge them to make that caring all inclusive in a personal way until it reaches every brother who has a need. The Church must teach its people to live together purposefully, planning action in terms of goals. It must guide them to act for the larger good, and to look thoughtfully at their actions, their weaknesses, and their accomplishments.

Christianity has always been a fellowship of believers. And Christians have always found power in that fellowship. The apostles went out with power and wrought more than any one of them alone would have dared to dream. They were united in a bond of consecration that had grown through the years of living, thinking, and working together with the Master.

A study of the Gospels and of Jesus' approach to men shows him to be a teacher who cared about persons. He loved persons and he sought to bring all men into the love of God. Many instances in the Gospels show how he knew his people, how he stimulated their thinking, how he turned the question back to them, how he related his teaching to the familiar, how he met people where they were.

The book of Acts is filled with the record of the deliberations of the apostles. It is a vivid account of a small group

166

working together. Each had his own responsibility and his own work, yet the group planned together and studied the effects of their work together.

Christianity is a movement of people who believe. It is a movement which finds power in diversity of thought but unity of spirit. Today needs disciples whose vision sees across the years, backward to recapture the power the apostles knew, and forward to see what the world may, through their efforts, under God, become.

The fellowship of Christians starts in the small group, the family, the Sunday-school class, the youth fellowship, and the committee or club. It is here that lives grow and develop. It is here that lives are changed and redirected. The small group, with its concern for individuals, is at the heart of all progress that is made toward good and God. The leader of such a group has the greatest opportunity in the world. It is a work that calls for both consecration and skill. The more deeply consecrated the leader, the more determined will he be to improve his skill.

It is Sunday morning. The sun in his travels from coast to coast touches first one spire and then another. The churches of our land stand forth in quiet splendor, assured and strong. Voices rise in joyful praise. Hands outstretch to clasp in brotherhood. Did we but rise to the full power of our fellowship, what a voice would fill the land!

BIBLIOGRAPHY

Association for Supervision and Curriculum Development. *Group Planning in Education.* Washington: National Education Association, 1945. Especially chs. xix and xx.
——. *Group Processes in Supervision.* Washington: National Education Association, 1948. Especially ch. ii.
Baxter, B. and Cassidy, R. *Group Experience the Democratic Way.* New York: Harper & Bros., 1943. Especially part I.
Coyle, Grace L. *Group Work with American Youth.* New York: Harper & Bros., 1948. Good discussion of relationship of leader's values to the group.
Cunningham, Ruth and Associates. *Understanding Group Behavior of Boys and Girls.* New York: Teachers College, Columbia University, 1951. Shows how sociometry helps in study of groups.
Haiman, Franklyn S. *Group Leadership and Democratic Action.* Boston: Houghton Mifflin Co., 1951. Very clear presentation of group and leadership.
Kilpatrick, William H. *Group Education for a Democracy.* New York: Association Press, 1940. Especially chs. viii and ix on learning.
Klein, Alan F. *Society, Democracy, and the Group.* New York: Woman's Press, 1953. Especially pp. 42-47 on the development of inner discipline.
Lane, Howard A. and Beauchamp, Mary. *Human Relations in Teaching.* New York: Prentice-Hall, Inc., 1955. An excellent study of human growth and group techniques in relation to teaching children.
Lotz, P. H., ed. *Orientation in Religious Education.* New York and Nashville: Abingdon Press, 1950. Especially articles by Mildred Eakin, "Newer Techniques in Teaching," pp. 197-206 and Harrison S. Elliott, "Individual and Group Counseling," pp. 183-96.
Murray, Clyde. *Guide Lines for Group Leaders.* New York: Whiteside, Inc., 1954. Especially the ten responsibilities of leaders, pp. 195 ff., and eight principles of group work.

Slavson, S. R. *Creative Group Education*. New York: Association Press, 1937. Good examples of groups at work.

Thelen, Herbert A. *Dynamics of Groups at Work*. Chicago: The University of Chicago Press, 1954. Thorough and readable.

Wilson, Gertrude and Ryland, Gladys. *Social Group Work Practice*. Boston: Houghton Mifflin Co., 1949. Especially part I.

Here is a book for *all* group leaders in the local church—from the kindergarten teacher to the church-school superintendent. The principles of group activity and democratic group leadership are put into practical terms for the average church-school teacher and leader of every age group.

Drawing illustrations from her years of experience and study in the field of group leadership, the author first examines working group situations at all age levels. She then discusses the objectives of Christian education, emphasizing that much of our learning takes place in group situations.

Dr. Douty next deals with group organization, the procedures and techniques of good group functioning, and the role of the leader and his preparations. Lastly, she looks at church-school superintendents, ministers, and directors of religious education as leaders of a group of workers, showing how they can build morale and help their teachers to grow and to do a better job.

Here is a practical book that may be effectively used by the individual teacher in a program of self-improvement, by a local church staff in a study group, or in a general leadership training course on group leadership.